Holy Living

Study

K. Kale Yu

Elaine A. Heath
General Editor

HOLY LIVING: STUDY

Copyright © 2019 by Abingdon Press.

All rights reserved

No part of this work may be reproduced or transmitted in any form or by any means, electronic or mechanical, including photocopying and recording, or by any information or retrieval system, except as may be expressly permitted in the 1976 Copyright Act or in writing from the publisher. Requests for permission should be addressed in writing to Permissions, The United Methodist Publishing House, 2222 Rosa L. Parks Blvd., Nashville, TN 37228 or e-mailed to permissions@umpublishing.org.

All Scripture quotations unless noted otherwise are taken from the New Revised Standard Version of the Bible, copyright 1989, Division of Christian Education of the National Council of the Churches of Christ in the United States of America. Used by permission. All rights reserved.

Scripture quotations marked KJV are from The Authorized (King James) Version. Rights in the Authorized Version in the United Kingdom are vested in the Crown. Reproduced by permission of the Crown's patentee, Cambridge University Press.

Scripture quotations marked AMPC are taken from the Amplified® Bible, Classic Edition, Copyright © 1954, 1958, 1962, 1964, 1965, 1987 by The Lockman Foundation. Used by permission. www.Lockman.org

Scripture quotations marked (GNT) are from the Good News Translation in Today's English Version- Second Edition © 1992 by American Bible Society. Used by Permission.

Scripture quotations marked NASB are taken from the *New American Standard Bible*®, Copyright © 1960, 1962, 1963, 1968, 1971, 1972, 1973, 1975, 1977, 1995 by The Lockman Foundation. Used by permission. (www.Lockman.org)

Scripture quotations marked NIV are taken from THE HOLY BIBLE, NEW INTERNATIONAL VERSION®, NIV® Copyright © 1973, 1978, 1984, 2011 by Biblica, Inc.™ Used by permission of Zondervan. All rights reserved worldwide.

Scripture quotations marked NKJV™ are taken from the New King James Version®. Copyright © 1982 by Thomas Nelson, Inc. Used by permission. All rights reserved.

Scripture quotations from *THE MESSAGE*. Copyright © by Eugene H. Peterson 1993, 1994, 1995, 1996, 2000, 2001, 2002. Used by permission of NavPress Publishing Group.

ISBN 9781501877643

Manufactured in the United States of America

19 20 21 22 23 24 25 26 27 28—10 9 8 7 6 5 4 3 2 1

ABINGDON PRESS
Nashville

TABLE OF CONTENTS

Dedication 4

Foreword 5

Introduction 7

Chapter 1: Knowing God 11

Chapter 2: The Surprising Things
We Did Not Know 39

Chapter 3: Growing Closer to God 69

Chapter 4: Study as Life-long Pursuit 99

Notes 128

To
Elli, Elgin, Ella, & Ellen
"This is eternal life, that they may know You."
John 17:3

FOREWORD

From the time that individuals began responding to Jesus' call to follow him, they began to learn rhythms of life that would be essential for them to be able to live their lives wholeheartedly for God. Chief among these practices was prayer. Jesus modeled for them how to withdraw from busy service to spend time alone in prayer. He offered prayer verbally in front of them, and when they asked, taught them to pray with the prayer we now call the Lord's Prayer. Following Jesus' ascension, as the disciples waited in Jerusalem "for what the Father had promised," that is, the Holy Spirit, Luke tells us that "all were united in their devotion to prayer" (Acts 1:4, 14). Prayer was foundational and formational, positioning them to receive the Holy Spirit, God's empowering presence that both indwelled and propelled them.

Following that transformative event, in due time they followed the Spirit's leading and bore witness to Jesus "to the end of the earth" (Acts 1:8). Their lives were busy, on the move, teaching, preaching, healing, explaining, encouraging, and confronting the evil and injustice of their society. Yet all of that doing, they knew, had to emanate from a deeply grounded experience of being. Nurturing a loving relationship with God was a central commitment that they, like we, had to learn to practice. Apart from this relationship, their

their busyness was meaningless. So they and those who followed them in the faith added to the practice of prayer a wide range of spiritual disciplines to strengthen their relationship with God, help them grow in Christlikeness, and fuel them for the work God called them to do.

Some of these practices—things like meditation, simplicity, and fasting—are more inwardly focused. Others are expressed outwardly and corporately—things like confession and worship. And some of the practices can be both, such as prayer. All of them—and there are many—work together to help us achieve lives of balance, anchored securely to Christ and equipped for meaningful engagement with others.

This book is one in a series, each volume focusing on a single discipline. In this volume, Kale K. Yu encourages us to realize that study as a spiritual practice helps us meet and experience God and deepen our faith in God. I challenge you to engage the practice of study so that you can experience the living God in new ways, enliven your faith, and ground yourself in God's word and God's ways.

Elaine A. Heath
General Editor

INTRODUCTION
Holy Living: Study

Botox injections have become common in cosmetic surgery. When injected, Botox paralyzes facial muscles, thus helping to remove wrinkles from a patient's face. Recently, a team of university researchers stumbled upon an unintended psychological side-effect of this treatment. Those who received Botox on the muscles that allow a person to frown were also happier and less anxious than those who left these muscles untreated. Because the muscles necessary to frown were paralyzed, patients could not physically frown anymore, and it made a significant difference to how they actually felt. Conversely, the research also showed that people who grimaced during uncomfortable procedures felt more pain than those who didn't.

The mere mention of the word *study* causes many of us to frown or grimace. It's not a word that exactly inspires excitement, but in order to fully embrace study as a spiritual practice, we need to see that it can be more than we think it is. Study as a spiritual practice is a far cry from what we did in school growing up. In contrast to a boring or academic exercise, study as a spiritual practice can be enriching, stimulating, and deeply imaginative.

When one Christian woman was asked the secret to her longevity on the occasion of her 114th birthday, she replied that she loves everything in life. She added that she has "no complaints" and that she wouldn't have been able to live this long if she had complained for 114 years. Today, our lives are immersed in so many negative images and words that it can be difficult to break free. In some ways, the spiritual discipline of study acts like an injection that paralyzes our negative feelings and impulses. Ultimately however, the spiritual practice of study helps us to meet God, experience God, and deepen our faith.

We'll start our exploration of this spiritual practice by challenging our preconceptions of study, shifting our understanding of what it means. We will realize that God wants us to study, not in order to gather trivial information, but in order to experience the power of the living God. There are many verses in the Bible that guide us to encounter God through study, and we may be surprised to learn how much the "knowledge of God" is stressed in the Bible.

Chapter 2 gets more personal as we explore the ways that study as a spiritual practice helps us discover more about ourselves. Study enlivens our faith by helping us realize that Christianity is not a dead religion but something vibrant and full of life. Study energizes our faith experience and offers us an opportunity to examine ourselves. When we question, engage, and encounter God in this way, it brings to the surface many of our personal concerns and questions.

Study as a spiritual practice also brings us closer to God. Chapter 3 examines how study shifts our attention away from a worldly focus that produces stress, anxiety, and uncertainty. The spiritual practice of study keeps us grounded in what God thinks rather than the fleeting affirmations that we too often chase. Study fills us with God's words; the more we study the more God's message fills our hearts and minds.

Since many of us are resistant to study, chapter 4 focuses on the discipline of study. Study must be undertaken as a long-term habit in order to fully enjoy its riches. We live in a culture that demands and expects instant results, but study as a spiritual practice requires patience. When we give it time, study produces character and strengthens our faith. It confirms our experience with God. This final chapter also considers practical steps that can help us make study become a regular habit.

Each chapter ends with Questions for Personal Reflection and Group Study. These are questions designed to encourage reflection and discussion, whether you are reading on your own or with a study group.

CHAPTER ONE
Knowing God

OPENING PRAYER
> My heart exults in the Lord;
>> my strength is exalted in my God.
> My mouth derides my enemies,
>> because I rejoice in my victory.
>
> There is no Holy One like the Lord,
>> no one besides you;
>> there is no Rock like our God.
> Talk no more so very proudly,
>> let not arrogance come from your mouth;
> for the Lord is a God of knowledge,
>> and by him actions are weighed.
>> (1 Samuel 2:1-3)

STUDY MORE, KNOW MORE

I'm sure a few of you picked up this book and immediately thought to yourself, "Study as a spiritual practice? Seriously? I didn't know study *was* a spiritual practice."

It's an easy reaction to understand and I get why some people might be hesitant. Study doesn't quite fit into the traditional mold of what people envision as a spiritual practice or spiritual discipline. In the popular imagination, a spiritual practice is a vision of serenity like a meditative pause during a stressful day or a soulful walk through a forest. Maybe your mind immediately goes to heartfelt prayers or the experience of Spirit-filled worship. For many of us, study is the farthest thing in our minds from a spiritual practice. Yet, at its heart, undertaking study as a spiritual practice helps us answer the fundamental question of how we can draw nearer to God and walk with God in our lives.

Wanting to know God more is a natural outgrowth of loving God. A desire to know God more is a desire to personally know the Creator who lovingly sent Jesus to save humanity. "[For my determined purpose is]," Paul declared, "that I may know Him." Knowing Christ is Paul's purpose in life, but just knowing about Jesus' work on the cross is not enough. For Paul, knowing Christ means that he must "[progressively become more deeply and intimately acquainted with Him, perceiving and recognizing and understanding the wonders of His Person more strongly and more clearly], and that I may in that same way," Paul adds, "come to know the power outflowing from His resurrection" (Philippians 3:10, AMPC, square brackets original).

Paul has an unquenchable desire to know Christ and wants the person of Christ to come alive in his life. Study as a spiritual practice is an essential way to explore who Christ is in the way Paul describes. By studying and developing this knowledge of God, we remember Christ and learn more about how this knowledge can shape our own lives.

Study is a spiritual practice, and this book will provide new insight into how to study better and more intentionally. However, understanding study as a spiritual practice is also different from the way we're used to studying. One big difference is that it is practical. Study is meant to be used, applied, and lived out. This may be a new concept that we need to get used to, especially since we, as comfortable passive observers, are becoming more comfortable with spending much of our time watching screens. Study calls and prepares us for something more.

PRACTICAL SKILLS

A minister and a soap maker were taking a walk one day when the soap maker said, "I don't understand the use of religion. Look at all the evil going on in the world! We've had two thousand years of Christianity and even after all these years of teaching about goodness, peace, and love, violence and misery are still with us. If religion is so good, why is it like this?"

The minister said nothing, and they continued on their walk down the street until they encountered a child playing in the dirt. Then the minister said, "Look at that child. You claim that soap makes people clean but look how dirty that child is. What good is soap? We've had soap in the world for thousands of years, and yet this child is absolutely filthy. I question if soap is effective at all."

The soap maker protested. "But, Reverend, soap cannot do any good unless it is used!"

It is not good enough to merely acknowledge the existence of soap or to learn about its ingredients, dimensions, and cleansing benefits. It needs to be used and applied generously. Religion works in the same way; studying who God is helps us develop the practical life skills required to walk alongside God. Study allows us to gain knowledge, confirmed through experience, that will enable us to live out our Christian faith in an intentional and purposeful way.

When put into practice, these skills, nurtured through regular practice, provide us with a sense of being and belonging. Through practical application of what the Christian learns, the Christian gains a clearer understanding of what it means to know Christ and to walk with him. At the conclusion of one parable, Jesus said, "Everyone then who hears these words of mine and acts on them will be like a wise man who built his house on rock. The rain fell, the floods came, and the winds blew and beat on that house, but it did not fall, because it had been founded on rock" (Matthew 7:24-25). By acting on God's word, the wise will take practical steps to apply God's teachings and thus build their houses on rock. The foolish, however, hear the words of Jesus, but do not act on them, and, in the process, build their houses on shifting sands.

YOU ARE CREATED TO KNOW GOD

God is inherently a relational being. This is most clearly revealed to us in the trinitarian nature of God— one God in three persons in an eternal relationship of love. This relational desire is also revealed in God's creation of humanity. God wants to be known by us in a personal and intimate way. Lifting his eyes upward to heaven, Jesus prayed, "This is eternal life, that they may *know* you, the only true God, and Jesus Christ whom you have sent" (John 17:3, emphasis added).

In the children's book, *I Can Read with My Eyes Shut!* Dr. Seuss wrote,

> The more that you read, the more things you will know.
> The more that you learn, the more places you'll go.[1]

We come with the mind-set of an explorer. We can't wait to discover what's next. We approach our study with anticipation that we will grow in the knowledge of God. Dr. Seuss was not writing about God, but the idea is similar. The more we study as a spiritual practice, the more things we will know. The more that we learn about God, the more places God will lead us. Study helps us develop "the mind of Christ" (1 Corinthians 2:16; see Philippians 4:7), and the practice challenges us to encounter new perspectives and insights.

We are not called to know God like a subject in a textbook, but to know and experience God in our hearts. When we studied in school, we were covering subjects like biology, literature, or history. For instance, if we were learning about the War of 1812, we would examine the political context of early nineteenth-century America, the conditions that led to war, and the motives and responses of the major players in the conflict. But learning about a topic from a textbook, while sometimes interesting, has little direct impact on our lives. Instead, the knowledge of God is powerful and alive. Paul wrote that God "desires everyone to be saved and to come to the knowledge of the truth" (1 Timothy 2:4).

In his letter to the Philippians, Paul wrote, "Finally, beloved, whatever is true, whatever is honorable, whatever is just, whatever is pure, whatever is pleasing, whatever is commendable, if there is any excellence and if there is anything worthy of praise, *think about these things*. Keep on doing the things that you have learned and received and heard and seen in me, and the God of peace will be with you" (Philippians 4:8-9, emphasis added).

To "think about these things" means that we should reflect, examine, and study them. In the Amplified, Classic Edition translation (AMPC), the phrase "think about these things" is translated as "think on and weigh and take account of these things [fix your mind on them]." *The Message* relates it as "filling your minds and meditating."

A quotation widely attributed to the Chinese sage, Confucius (551-479 BC), says this about learning, "By three methods we may learn wisdom: first, by reflection which is noblest; second, by imitation which is easiest; and third, by experience which is the bitterest." Undertaking study as a spiritual practice provides us with an opportunity to mull over any passage of Scripture and reflect on the parts, connections, and dynamics. We consider what is being emphasized and for what reasons. We seek to understand how the emotional intensity of the language reinforces a particular point.

From a biblical standpoint, the Christian is called to have an active mind, constantly engaged in examining what is good, true, and excellent (see Romans 12:2). When we embrace study as a spiritual practice, we approach it with a desire to discover and examine insights with which to weigh our Christian understanding. In Isaiah 44:18-19, the people are condemned for lack of understanding and knowledge, "They do not know, nor do they comprehend; for their eyes are shut, so that they cannot see, and their minds as well, so that they cannot understand. No one considers, nor is there knowledge or discernment."

The word *study* also suggests a repeated examination of a particular topic. We do not study material that we read for leisure such as magazines, novels, or news stories. We simply read them one time and put them aside. To study something, we approach it with more seriousness, and we revisit the material over and over again to ensure that we have comprehended it as much as we can. That is the attitude we bring to the practice of study and that is the attitude that comes from a desire to know the living God. In Ephesians 4:11-14, Paul describes how different gifts in the church have been appointed so that "all of us come to the unity of the faith and of the *knowledge of the Son of God*, to maturity, to the measure of the full stature of Christ" (emphasis added).

GETTING TO KNOW GOD

My fourth-grade daughter came home one day to share with me about a girl in class who is "so nice." I teased her a bit and asked her, "Ella, is there anyone you know who isn't nice?" She had to think about that for a moment. "Well," she said, "not really, but there's this boy who is really annoying!" On the surface, everyone seems nice; or as someone once said, "Everyone seems normal until you get to know them." When we get a close-up, however, we notice the details. When we take the time to know people and see them beyond appearances, we may be amazed at what we find.

From afar, God can come across as a friendly stranger. Benevolent and loving, sure, but disconnected from our world. If we do not take steps to know God at a deeper level, God will remain a stranger to us. We are called to know God in a rich and more fulfilling way. If we get to know God, we will be surprised by what we discover. We may even find that the more we know about God, the more we want to learn.

What is incredible is that God wants to be known by us as well. Think about that for a moment. The Most High God, the Almighty, the Creator, wants us to know and experience who God is! The Lord of the universe invites us to step forward into the practice of study, which provides a way to do this.

Some of us are afraid or intimidated to approach God. We may have been taught at an early age to maintain a safe distance from God, lest we make a mistake or cause offense. If we have any inhibitions, reluctance, or barriers between us and God, feel confident that God wants us to pursue, seek, and ask. In Hebrews 4, the writer declares: "Since, then, we have a great high priest who has passed through the heavens, Jesus, the Son of God, let us hold fast to our confession" (v. 14). Because of Jesus, we have access to the throne of God! We are instructed to step forward into God's presence. "Let us therefore approach the throne of grace with boldness, so that we may receive mercy and find grace to help in time of need" (v. 16).

THROUGH THE FOG

One day, an excited young pilot who had just received his wings was flying a small commercial flight to Boston. As the plane was passing through Rhode Island on its way to Boston, a heavy fog descended on the region. The young pilot had learned to trust the plane's instrument panel in a situation like this, but he was still worried about the landing. He knew how to land a plane, but he had never had to land in such dense fog.

Not only that, he was scheduled to land at one of the busiest airports in the country, and the truth of the matter was that he was not familiar with the layout. As he thought about his predicament, he started to break out in cold sweat.

"What will I do? How will I do it?"

Then, the pilot heard the voice of the air traffic controller. "Because of this dense fog, I am going to put you on a holding pattern," he crackled over the radio.

The pilot quietly thought to himself, "Hallelujah!" This person at the air traffic control would now be guiding voice.

For the next 45 minutes, the controller gently guided the pilot through the blinding fog. As the voice in the tower told him where to adjust and turn, the young pilot realized the controller was guiding him around obstacles and away from potential collisions.

When we engage in study as a spiritual practice, we are like the pilot, and God is the air traffic controller. As we dig into Scripture, we may feel a bit lost and confused, like we are descending into a heavy fog, but the air traffic controller's voice guides us through the journey.

As we dive into the practice of study, we need to trust God's voice in the process. Through this, we become open to the Holy Spirit leading us through the fog, and we admit that we do not have all the answers. A vital part of this practice is understanding that we go about our studies in partnership with God. This is a two-way interaction in which we trust God to speak into our situations, our issues, and our questions.

It is likely that trusting God as we study will not come easily to many of us. We will need to re-orient ourselves to accept the idea that God is working alongside us during this process and that, through our study, we are lifting God up in order to worship God and to receive holy insights. Study as a spiritual practice works best when we allow ourselves to trust God's word and allow ourselves to be moved by the Spirit.

THE KNOWLEDGE OF GOD

Everyone has been through something difficult during their life that has made it more difficult to trust others. Yet we are called to trust in God. In order to study God and know God in a deeper way, we need to expand our trust and take a leap of faith. We must believe that God has our best interests in mind.

The blessed privilege of being a Christian comes from knowing Christ in a deeply personal and trusting way. It is important to understand our shortcomings and take small steps toward trusting God more. We must overcome our pain and realize that our life is made richer by fully trusting in Christ. As we open our hearts more, we can grow in our knowledge of Christ.

In Colossians 1:9, Paul tells us that he and other Christian leaders "have not ceased praying" for the believers "and asking that you may be filled with the knowledge of God's will in all spiritual wisdom and understanding." Addressing the believers, Paul urges them to increase in the knowledge of God "so that you may lead lives worthy of the Lord, fully pleasing to him, as you bear fruit in every good work and as you grow in the knowledge of God" (v. 10).

Paul does not ask that the believers get *some* knowledge or even *a lot* of knowledge. Instead, he asks that Christians be "filled" with the knowledge of God that will lead to "all spiritual wisdom and understanding." The knowledge of God translates to action as it will guide believers to live "worthy of the Lord, fully pleasing to him."

We were made to know God—to not only believe in God but also passionately experience God as eyewitnesses to God's majesty and power. This pursuit of knowing God fills the deepest needs of the human heart.

In John 17:25-26, Jesus continues this theme, "Righteous Father, the world does not know you, but I know you; and these know that you have sent me. I made your name known to them, and I will make it known, so that the love with which you have loved me may be in them, and I in them."

Paul desires that Christians have "all the riches of assured understanding and have the knowledge of God's mystery, that is, Christ himself, in whom are hidden all the treasures of wisdom and knowledge" (Colossians 2:2-3).

Many of us may be wondering how knowledge leads to all these things. There is an element of mystery to this.

> The moment one definitely commits oneself, then Providence moves too. Whatever you think you can do, or believe you can do, begin it. Action has magic, power and grace.[2]

DEFINING STUDY AS A SPIRITUAL PRACTICE

The kind of study we did in school and the concept of study as a spiritual practice are not the same. There are similarities, but fundamentally, study as a spiritual practice is a search for spiritual renewal, which I'm sure we can agree was not the central purpose of our studies in school.

At its root, study is the effort to acquire knowledge about a subject through reading, research, and analysis. A big reason why people are often unenthusiastic about study is the word *effort*.

Studying requires mental effort to examine and analyze material that we may find abstract, difficult, or incomprehensible. Concentrating on one topic so intensely can intimidate some people.

Yet, if we can change the way we think about study, we can re-envision it as a positive struggle. The struggle of study can become an enjoyable exercise. All of us know about the good things that have come about from struggles we've faced in our lives. We would not be walking we had not struggled through countless failed attempts as a toddler. If we had given up after a few days, we would have never enjoyed the ability to walk, jump, or run.

The NBA's Philadelphia 76ers know a thing or two about struggling. During a three-year stretch starting in 2013, the team was simply awful. A newspaper headline asked the obvious question, "Philadelphia 76ers: Worst Team of All Time?" They were so bad that, over the three years, they lost more games than any other team and broke the NBA's record for consecutive games lost.

As you can imagine, fans were having fits. Sportswriters called the team an "abomination" and an "atrocity," but Sam Hinkie, the General Manager who was hired to oversee the franchise, stuck to his plan and encouraged fans to "trust the process." Few could have envisioned at the time (except perhaps Hinkie) that the dark years of struggle would bear tremendous fruit.

During the abysmal years, Hinkie carefully assembled players with extraordinary potential. With a core of exceptional talent, acquired during the lowest point of the franchise, the 76ers have now positioned themselves to contend for championships for many years to come. Fans who understood Hinkie's grand vision in the beginning were happy that the team aimed to transcend mediocrity, but they also knew they had to suffer through the growing pains. The team was finally "thinking long-term at [the] expense of any short-term gains."[3]

Good things can come from struggle, and study is no exception. Study allows space for us to struggle with our questions, problems, and concerns.

A story may help us to see that sometimes struggle is beneficial and necessary. A woman was walking through the woods when she noticed a cocoon dangling from a tree branch. When she took the cocoon home, she noticed a small opening. She was delighted to see the little butterfly as it began to emerge from the cocoon.

She watched the butterfly for several hours as it struggled to force its body through the little hole. The little butterfly kept at for hours with no success. Nothing happened. It seemed exhausted and didn't go any further.

She wanted to help the butterfly, so she found a pair of scissors in the house and carefully snipped off more from the top of the cocoon, making a larger hole for the little butterfly. With the larger hole, the butterfly emerged easily, but its body was swollen and small and its wings were underdeveloped. She thought the butterfly would fly any second, but it never could.

She learned only later that the hours of struggle it takes to push through the small hole and emerge from the cocoon enable the butterfly to fully develop its wings. All the fluid in the wings is squeezed out during the push. Once the butterfly squeezes itself out of the cocoon, it is strong enough to soar and fly away.

It was necessary for the butterfly to struggle in order to achieve flight. Any shortcuts undercut the butterfly's ability to achieve its fullest potential. Life is full of struggle, but we need not be afraid of them.

When we watch a movie or browse the internet, it is a passive experience. We are not debating with the content or critically analyzing the novel. In other words, we are mostly on the receiving end of the shows, sports events, entertainment, or news. Study, however, is proactive and requires our mental energies to be engaged in order to acquire knowledge through information. The acquisition of dense concepts and ideas can be particularly frustrating as it requires more mental effort.

However, acquiring knowledge, while difficult, doesn't have to be boring or unpleasant. We have gotten so used to the idea of studying as a tedious affair that we find it strange to suggest that studying could be exciting.

It would be easy for students to develop a resistance to study. One fourth-grader brought a note to his teacher. Upon reading, it was obvious that the note was written by the student. It read, "Please excuse Sam from reading and other assignments because he doesn't like studying."

Given our frustrating experiences with studying, it is difficult for people to imagine study as having any redeeming spiritual value. In the minds of many, study feels distant and forced. The fact that we were graded for our study made it worse, as getting low grades affects our self-worth and confidence.

Happily, there is no grading or judgment when we study as a spiritual practice. Instead, we approach study as a heart-to-heart conversation between us and God.

NEW WINESKINS FOR STUDY

In order to succeed at the spiritual practice of study, we must throw out our preconceived notions of study and instill a new understanding. In the parable of the wineskins, Jesus refers to the nonsense of pouring new wine into old wineskins. In that time, goat skins were the ancient version of water bottles. These skins, cut and sewn into containers in the shape of a kidney, held various liquids such as water, olive oil, milk, and of course, wine.

Wine in the wineskin would ferment and cause the skins to expand. Wineskins that had already expanded would not be able to stretch any further. Therefore, it didn't make any sense for anyone to pour new wine into old wineskins. If they did "the new wine will burst the skins and will be spilled, and the skins will be destroyed" (Luke 5:37).

Jesus tells us that, instead, "New wine must be put into fresh wineskins" (v. 38). It is difficult to pour in new, refreshing knowledge when we are using old, tired notions that will not allow the new content to expand and renew our hearts and minds.

Unlike our studies in school, no one is pushing us to do this work. Our new endeavor to study is voluntary. We are studying because we want to. The spiritual practice of study should not produce anxiety or stress. There is no teacher grading you, and there is no test.

Some of you may be thinking, "I haven't studied in years! I am so rusty. I don't think I can study at this point." It is never too late to study.

Consider the story of a 70-year old inmate in California. The man had never graduated from high school, but late in his life he decided to finally earn his General Education Diploma (GED). It wasn't easy, and he failed the first time.

In fact, he failed the first few times. After ten years, he finally passed the test and received his GED. But he didn't stop there. While behind bars, he enrolled in college classes at a local community college that offers long-distance learning courses to inmates. When a reporter asked him why he was pursuing higher education at this stage in his life, the man simply remarked, "Well, why not?" He went on, "It's good to (learn) what you don't know. I have the motivation, the enthusiasm, the inspiration and the tools to work with."[4]

"Well, why not?" That is a good response to many of our excuses. This man has new wineskins. He is ready, motivated, and excited to study.

To help some of our resistance to studying, consider some of these old wineskins that we need to replace.

Old Wineskin #1: "I have no time! There isn't enough time in my day."

This may be the mind-set many of us start out with. Who has time for anything new nowadays? Our schedules are filled to the brim; for many people, there isn't any time available. However, we also know that there's always something we can cut back on. Maybe it's TV or social media. It might be difficult to reduce our time doing these things, but we need to make time to study. The practice of study requires us to be intentional, and we can make time for things that are important.

Old Wineskin #2: "I hate studying!"

In our culture, studying is unfortunately seen as unpleasant, boring, or even tortuous. Many of us feel that studying is something we need to be liberated from, not something to be embraced. It's important for us to realize, however, that, when we study, we are empowered to learn and grow. Instead of being liberated from study, study itself liberates us from many of the things that constrain our lives. We may think we hate studying, but we must also acknowledge that in the right circumstances we can grow to love it.

Old Wineskin #3: "Studying is not fun!"

Let's face it, studying while growing up was not always fun. We sat through classes that force-fed information to us. We got scolded by our parents when our grades slipped. In college, we faced assignments, mountains of books, and essays. We stayed up all night in caffeine-induced sprints to finish a 20-page final paper. We have, unfortunately, had it drilled into us that studying is a tremendous bore.

That's not the same for the spiritual practice of study. No one is judging us here or criticizing us for our failures to grasp a concept. There are no limits to what we can learn or when we can learn it. Instead of being a bore, the spiritual practice of study is a privilege that allows us to draw nearer to God.

Old Wineskin #4: "Study has little or no spiritual value."

Growing up, we were accustomed to a limited and specific kind of study. This kind of study dealt almost exclusively with our rational powers. Our society regards rationality as the chief source and test of knowledge.

We need to consider how this way of thinking limits us. Study as we experienced it growing up was empty of spiritual direction, presence, and inspiration. Few of us can say that our formal education affirmed our spiritual selves and nourished our moral conscience. Study was not about spiritual values or development, but rather passing a series of exams or getting a degree that would land us a good job.

This is not the case for the spiritual practice of study. Instead, we don't use study to make ourselves more marketable, but to develop ourselves. We are learning in order to challenge ourselves and grow, not conform to someone else's measures or needs. When we look at study this way, we can see it as an opportunity for spiritual growth, and not the way we viewed it when we were younger.

BEYOND RATIONALISM

When we study as a spiritual practice, we dive deeper into the heart of Jesus' message.

In John 4:1-42, we are told that Jesus struck up a conversation with a Samaritan woman who came to a well to draw water. After a short conversation, Jesus tells her that he can give her "living water." Quickly perceiving that Jesus means something beyond ordinary water, the woman asks, "Where do you get that living water" (v. 11)? Although she is curious about what Jesus means, she expresses doubt and skepticism.

Jesus responds, "Everyone who drinks of this water will be thirsty again, but those who drink of the water that I will give them will never by thirsty. The water that I will give will become in them a spring of water gushing up to eternal life" (v. 14).

The people in ancient Palestine knew all about springs. The Gihon Spring, for example, was the main source of fresh water for the city of Jerusalem for more than 5,000 years, up until the twentieth century. In Hebrew, *gihon* is a term that translates to "gushing," and the spring continues to gush out water for tourists today.

When Jesus speaks of a "spring of water gushing up," the woman's ears perk up, and she replies, "Sir, give me this water, so that I may never be thirsty or have to keep coming here to draw water" (v. 15). Jesus proceeds to expand her understanding of a gushing spring to illustrate the life-giving water he offers to people. Jesus concludes, "God is spirit, and those who worship him must worship in spirit and truth" (v. 24).

The spiritual practice of study aims to generate a genuine, heartfelt emotional response that touches the soul. A rationalistic approach may convince our cognitive side, but seldom does it reach deep inside and excite the heart the way it did to the Samaritan woman at the well when she pleaded, "Give me this water."

Just as the interaction with Jesus provokes the woman's creative sensibilities, study will likewise enlarge our creative powers and will stir invention, insight, and greater perspective.

INFORMATION AND KNOWLEDGE

Before we go further, we should consider the differences between *information* and *knowledge*. One of the problems of modern society is that we are drowning in information. Our technology has brought unprecedented access to us and with it an avalanche of information. With just a few taps on our phones, we can search for anything and easily find all available information. On one hand, the easy availability of information is super-convenient when we need practical information on how to do things, like how to make chicken noodle soup. I do not know what I would do without Google Maps to help me navigate through out-of-town trips.

On the other hand, this flood of information can be overwhelming. Just searching the word *spiritual* on Amazon will lead to a dizzying array of perspectives from all over the religious and quasi-religious spectrum. When considering the deeply meaningful aspects of our lives, this "too-much-information" environment can be unhelpful. In fact, it may lead to even greater confusion and insecurity.

An article in the *National Defense Magazine* reported that the US Defense Department has spent billions of dollars on hardware that amass an immense amount of information. "Those systems create avalanches of data that clog military information networks and overwhelm analysts." According to the article, "Intelligence experts say the military is drowning in data."[5]

When we are swarmed with data, it can be difficult to sift and sort through everything to determine what is useful and what is not. It can distract us and leave us frustrated. This avalanche of information is like floating in the vastness of an ocean. In every direction we turn, all we see is water and sky. Which way do we go? How do we determine what to do?

Knowledge, however, is like the rudder on a boat. The rudder guides the boat through the ocean to a certain destination. Without the rudder, the boat is helpless and will drift aimlessly at the whim of the ocean's waves.

Information is the endless ocean; knowledge guides us through the waves and the storms to our destination. All kinds of information is out there; knowledge gives us a framework for understanding our world. Knowledge makes sense of the confusion by synthesizing information into coherent parts.

Having knowledge of something or someone is a higher level of understanding and certainty. It can also indicate intimacy and a deeper relationship. In addition, knowledge implies a unity of thought that helps us to decipher our world.

That intimacy is illustrated when we compare having information about God to having knowledge of

God. Having knowledge of God expresses a personal relationship that is based on experience. Knowledge is a deep understanding that has moral, spiritual, and experiential implications. Knowledge is gained through familiarity, awareness, study, and experience.

STUDY AS ASKING QUESTIONS

Albert Einstein once said, "The important thing is not to stop questioning."[6] The spiritual practice of study is an opportunity to ask God questions.

It's important to note that asking God questions is not the same as questioning God. Questioning God implies that we are unsure of God's decisions and actions. In some situations, this may make sense. Job, for instance, questions God, but it comes from a place of uncertainty or even doubt. Even with affirmation we may still be unsure of the answers in this kind of questioning.

However, God encourages us to ask questions to engage our faith and help with our faith formation. Jesus encouraged his followers, "Ask, and it will be given you; search, and you will find; knock, and the door will be opened for you. For everyone who asks receives, and everyone who searches finds, and for everyone who knocks, the door will be opened" (Matthew 7:7).

When we come before God with an open heart and a willingness to learn and grow in faith, God answers our prayers to increase in knowledge and understanding. When the angel Gabriel appeared before Mary, the angel said something to her that did not make sense at the moment: "And now, you will conceive in your womb and bear a son" (Luke 1:31). Stunned by the news, Mary questioned, "How can this be, since I am a virgin" (v. 34)?

I have encountered many Christians who think that they are not supposed to ask God questions—almost as if God will be offended by our intrusion. They really feel that they shouldn't take up God's time with what they think of as petty requests. Other Christians have an attitude that God is to be worshiped to a point where asking God questions seems disrespectful. This could not be further from the truth. Paul instructed Christians, "in everything by prayer and supplication with thanksgiving let your requests be made known to God (Philippians 4:6)."

A second-grade teacher was reviewing math symbols and drew on the board the greater-than symbol (>) and the less-than sign (<). She then turned to her students and asked, "Does anyone remember what these symbols are?" An excited student responded, "One means fast-forward and the other means rewind." If she didn't ask the question, then she would never have known to correct them.

It's important to keep asking questions with an open heart to learn and discover. Asking God questions helps us to draw closer to God. Someone once said, "Successful people ask better questions, and as a result, they get better answers." God urges us to ask, seek, search, dig, and whatever else to go deeper in our understanding.

Study as a spiritual practice is an opportunity to engage in a serious conversation of our deepest questions. In turn, God will respond because we ask these questions with a spirit of humility and a sincere desire to know.

KNOWLEDGE, EXPERIENCE, AND MORAL ACTION

In dismay, the psalmist cries out,

> Have they no knowledge, those evildoers,
>   who eat up my people as they eat bread,
>   and do not call upon God? (Psalm 53:4)

According to the psalmist, the evil being done is the result of an absence of knowledge. This may confuse some readers. How exactly does the lack of knowledge lead to someone doing evil?

The author of Proverbs tells us how the knowledge of God strengthens the moral framework of the believer. In Proverbs 23:12, the author writes, "Apply your mind to instruction / and your ear to words of knowledge." At the same time, the lack of knowledge has the effect of clouding people's moral vision. As we noted earlier, Isaiah underscores this failure: "They do not know, nor do they comprehend; for their eyes are shut, so that they cannot see, and their minds as well, so that they cannot understand. No one considers, nor is there knowledge or discernment" (Isaiah 44:18-19).

An important part of our practice of study is internalizing the idea that study helps form and shape our moral outlook. As a spiritual practice, study is a creative process that touches our souls. In some ways, studying is like practicing our lines before we go on stage to perform. We allow the lines to shape our thoughts and emotions, then, when we are on stage, we say the lines with the conviction and passion necessary to convey these emotions. Study enables us to recite our moral lines, internalize them, and then express them to others. As the saying goes, "Knowledge is of no value unless you put it into practice."

STUDY

A sports reporter once learned an important lesson about how practice can directly impact the outcome of a game when he interviewed Michael Jordan, widely considered the best basketball player of all-time. The reporter asked Jordan about the last shot of the 1998 NBA Finals. Many have called it one of the greatest plays in NBA history. Jordan's team, the Chicago Bulls, were down by one with only 5.2 second left on the clock. Jordan took the ball, went down the court and sunk the game-winning shot to put the Bulls ahead and clinch their sixth championship win of his career.

This shot was full of pressure. Jordan's team was down. Time was running-out. The championship was on the line. Yet, when the reporter asked him about how he felt before he took the shot, Jordan said he felt little pressure.

Before the game, the reporter had watched the Bulls practice and he was amazed. This practice session was nothing the type of practice he was used to or that we might imagine. There was no goofing off, no half-speed play; instead the Bulls' practice was like a real game with all of its intensity, emotion, and physicality. They pushed, shoved, and yelled at each other. In the middle of the action was Jordan, barking at his teammates louder than anyone.

After the practice was finished, the reporter expressed astonishment at how the Bulls could practice like that. Unmoved by the comment, Jordan responded, "Every day in practice was like that." The reporter asked why the Bulls pushed themselves so much during practice. Jordan answered, "So, when the game comes, there wasn't anything that I haven't already practiced."

Sometimes, Jordan said, practices were harder and tougher than the real games. When the actual game started, there was nothing that Jordan hadn't already seen and prepared for. Whatever plays, strategies, or traps the other team devised, Jordan was ready for anything.

The reporter then asked Jordan if fear of failure motivated his play. Jordan confided that fear was not a factor because he put in the work. He continued, "Work ethic eliminates fear." If you put in the work, what is there to fear? You know what you are capable of doing.[7]

Like Michael Jordan, when we study, we are practicing for the real game of life. The more we study, the more we know; the more we know, the more it shapes our moral actions and responses in the world. When we study, we prepare ourselves for anything.

The idea that the knowledge of God will lead to moral action may sound a bit strange. We are accustomed to thinking of knowledge as facts, data, or philosophies. These things don't necessarily have a direct effect on our moral sensibilities. However, when we dig down into how we understand knowledge, we will discover that this is not the case.

The separation of moral responsibility from knowledge derives from the ancient Greek understanding of knowledge. In their view, knowledge was sought for its own sake. This has flowed down over the centuries and filtered into the way many of us view academic knowledge. A sociologist, for instance, observes a tribal village or a group of teenagers. The observer can gain detailed knowledge of the subjects, but that does not necessarily mean the observer has a moral obligation to aid them. The primary objective was the knowledge itself.

Now, what if we put to a work a different understanding of knowledge. While the Greek understanding of knowledge comes from a detached, neutral, and intellect-based perspective, the Hebrew concept of knowledge possesses an obligation to respond to what we know; to know means being a participant and not merely an observer from the sidelines.

Knowledge, for the Hebrew people, also carried a weight of moral responsibility. In other words, knowledge prompted you into action. From a Hebrew perspective, knowledge placed expectations on the individual. To know something meant that a person had the moral and ethical demand to act on that knowledge.

The Hebrew concept of knowledge also held that knowledge has relational implications. The Hebrew mind-set was concerned with right conduct. The Greek mind-set, by comparison, was concerned with right thinking. For the Hebrew, knowledge was only knowledge if it was experienced by practicing and living it out.

These relational and experiential aspects of the Hebrew concept of knowing are expressed early in the book of Genesis. In Genesis 4:1, we are told that "The man knew his wife Eve, and she conceived and bore Cain." The Hebrew word used in that context was *yada* (עדי), or "to know." This is where we get the jokes about "knowing someone in the Biblical sense," but it also gets at the deeper connection, both relationally and experientially, of what it means "to know" in the Hebrew language.

To an observer, knowledge appears distant, passive, and detached. To a participant, knowledge is the gateway to a transformation of the whole person. It is to be in the game and to be an important part of the outcome.

We have an illustration of this kind of knowledge from Paul when he declared in Philippians 3:7-11:

> Yet whatever gains I had, these I have come to regard as loss because of Christ. More than that, I regard everything as loss because of the surpassing value of *knowing* Christ Jesus my Lord. For his sake I have suffered the loss of all things, and I regard them as rubbish, in order that I may gain Christ and be found in him, not having a righteousness of my own that comes from the law, but one that comes through faith in Christ, the righteousness from God based on faith. I want to *know* Christ and the power of his resurrection and the sharing of his sufferings by becoming like him in his death, if somehow I may attain the resurrection from the dead. (emphasis added)

When Paul mentions "the surpassing value of knowing Christ Jesus my Lord," one gets a sense that what he means more than intellectual knowledge, that is, understanding Jesus merely as a historical figure. Paul's knowledge of Christ is not limited to understanding Jesus intellectually. In knowing Christ, Paul is describing an emotional and spiritual encounter.

When Paul says, "I want to know Christ," he also mentions "the power" that comes with knowing Christ. In other words, knowing Christ is more than just thinking about a subject. Knowing Christ, in the way that Paul describes, generates power and authority of unsurpassed value.

Paul has discovered something so awesome that all the suffering that he endured previously seems like garbage in comparison. His prior hardship is nothing to him when thinking about what he has obtained in the process to "gain Christ and be found in him." To Paul, Christ is not like a person in history books. Knowing Christ is a profound personal experience that

STUDY

inspires Paul to a higher level of commitment. The knowledge of God stirs within us and opens a pathway to understand our world. God's words become alive, and we experience God participating in our lives.

Questions for Personal Reflection and Group Discussion

1. What first comes to your mind when you think about study as a kind of spiritual practice? What associations do you make with study? What do you think the spiritual practice of study looks like?

2. What does it mean that we are created to know God? How does knowledge of God shape our faith? What kind of knowledge helps us to grow closer to God?

3. What obstacles to study are the biggest obstacles for you? What concerns you? How can your community help you to overcome these obstacles?

4. What is the difference between *information* and *knowledge*? How do we use information to create knowledge? Is there such a thing as too much information? What about too much knowledge?

5. How does knowledge guide us to make better decisions in our life? How does it shape our moral actions?

CHAPTER 2

The Surprising Things We Did Not Know

OPENING PRAYER

For learning about wisdom and instruction,
for understanding words of insight,
for gaining instruction in wise dealing,
righteousness, justice, and equity;
to teach shrewdness to the simple,
knowledge and prudence to the young—
let the wise also hear and gain in learning,
and the discerning acquire skill,

. . . .

The fear of the Lord is the beginning of knowledge;
fools despise wisdom and instruction.

(Proverbs 1:2-5,7)

SPIRITUAL NUTRIENTS

In 2011, *Scientific American* published an article titled "Dirt Poor: Have Fruits and Vegetables Become Less Nutritious?" which revealed that our food today contains fewer nutrients than in the past. Fruits and vegetables harvested decades ago were much richer in vitamins and minerals than the ones we consume today.

One reason for the decline is the mass industrialization of food production, which has led to an increased usage of chemical fertilizers and pesticides.

Both the use of these chemicals and the general over-use of soil have stripped the soil of its natural, rich nutrients. "Sadly," reports the article, "each successive generation of fast-growing, pest-resistant carrot is truly less good for you than the one before."

A secondary reason, and a much more concerning trend, is the increased consumption of processed food, which is often nutrient-deficient. In a quest for speed and efficiency, many of us have replaced the nutrient rich foods of the past with quicker options with significantly less value to our health.[1]

In a similar way, our spiritual lives have also become nutrient deficient. We live in age where we are assaulted by distractions, temptations, and worldly offerings. These provide a momentary thrill, some kind of satisfaction for our spiritual hunger, but they do not fortify us or make us healthier. Instead, they simply entice us to come back for more and more. In my life, I've seen the world go from a place with no internet, no cell phones, and a number of TV channels you could count on one hand to an era with an unlimited buffet of viewing options and the never-ending distraction of ever-present connection sitting in your pocket.

It's only too obvious that there are a lot of options with little to no spiritual value in our world. Study presents us with a healthy alternative. It's doesn't appeal to us like a pizza or a steak, but it will sustain and strengthen us from the inside-out. However, since it appears less appealing at first, it requires discipline on our part to overcome other temptations begging for our attention.

In 1 Corinthians 3:2, Paul lamented that, while he wished he could feed the Christians more complex and stronger food, they "were not ready for solid food." Studying the Scripture is a first step in eating this solid food, and the more we do it, the more comfortable we become with it.

Our challenge is not to be satisfied with the simple things that we were given when we were "infants in Christ" (v. 1). Paul was excited for them to grow deeper in Christ, but he was also frustrated by their inability to take the next step: "Even now you are still not ready, for you are still of the flesh" (vv. 2-3). God desires to impart a greater and deeper knowledge to us, but we must take steps to study diligently in preparation to receive it.

DIVINE KNOWLEDGE

Jonathan Edwards (1703–1758), the Puritan luminary who helped spark the Great Awakening, understood fully the importance of Christians feeding on "solid food." In his sermon, "The Importance and Advantage of a Thorough Knowledge of Divine Truth" Edwards described "solid food" as the ability "to understand those things in divinity which are more abstruse and difficult to be understood, and which require great skill in things of this nature."[2] Edwards exhorted believers to develop a love of learning divine things and rejected the notion that study was the exclusive domain of theologians and ministers.

Instead, Edwards believed that each Christian was personally responsible for maturing in their faith and knowledge of God. "Every Christian," Edwards exhorted, "should make a business of endeavoring to grow in knowledge of divinity."[3] The Puritans of the Massachusetts Bay Colony, who founded Harvard College in 1636, understood the significance of study as a Christian discipline, so much so that they codified it into law. The Law of 1647 required towns of fifty families to hire a schoolmaster who would teach children to read and write so that they could begin understanding divine truth.

Methodist Circuit Riders, who rode across the American frontier preaching and evangelizing, also viewed learning as a vital component of Christian development. New converts were called to study what it meant to be a Christian through printed literature, such as tracts, sermons, religious magazines, and biographies of notable Christians. Through reading and study, these converts were called to deepen their faith and grow in their knowledge of God.

JOHN WESLEY AND STUDY

In the small collection, *Minutes of Several Conversations Between the Rev. Mr. Wesley and Others*, a fellow pastor asked John Wesley, "Why are we not more knowing?"[4] Wesley replied first with a short answer, "Because we are idle." Both idleness and busyness posed a considerable danger to Christians according to Wesley. He then added, "We must, absolutely must, cure this evil, or betray the cause of God."

But how are we to cure ourselves? Once again Wesley has an answer, "Read the most useful books, and that regularly and constantly. Steadily spend all the morning in the employ, or at least, five hours in four-and-twenty."

In the *Conversations*, Wesley responds to various statements of resistance to reading. To, "But I have no taste for reading," Wesley responded, "Contract a taste for it by use, or return to your trade." That's right, Wesley said that the pastor should either develop a love of reading or quit ministry and go back to his old job. Another objection was, "But I have no books."

No problem, replied Wesley. "I will give each of you [books]," Wesley added, "as fast as you will read them."

Yet another pastor told Wesley that he doesn't read books but "*only* the Bible." That was acceptable to Wesley, but, if you choose to read only the Bible, "Then you ought to teach others to read only the Bible, and, by parity of reason, to *hear only* the Bible."

Finally, someone mentioned to Wesley a Christian who "neither reads the Bible, nor anything else." "This," according to Wesley, "is rank enthusiasm," in other words, a kind of Christianity that is completely dependent on emotional appeal without the assistance of knowledge.

Over and over again, we see Wesley return to the same theme. Reading is important. Study is important. If we want to know God, we must continue to dig deeper and deeper into both the word of God and what the community of believers has learned from their own studies.

MAKE TIME TO STUDY

Even if we cultivate this desire to study, we may discover that we have little room in our schedules. For many of us, the days are already filled to the brim and we may have difficulty carving out the necessary time for study. The amount of time each of us can commit to study will vary from person to person, but we should all commit at least an hour each week. If we are serious about engaging in study, we need to squeeze in time the same way that we do for exercise or any other important item on our schedule.

In order to make time for study, we may need to scale back on other things that consume our time. Think about your average week and take an inventory of your schedule. Where do you spend most of your time? According to a study conducted by USC, in 2017 Americans spent 23.6 hours per week online, nearly an entire day per week.[5] This represented a new high, and it has likely been exceeded yet again in the past few years. Given the many hours we spend on screens each week, this is one area where we can scale back and find a few hours to study.

It's important that we approach the practice of study fully committed, otherwise it can easily fall by the wayside. As you look at your calendar, see where you can make an appointment with yourself on a weekly basis. If you feel studying with others will keep you accountable, talk to your friends about forming a small study group together. Meet at a local coffee shop or diner and study different passages of Scripture or specific themes. As an example, C.S. Lewis, J.R.R. Tolkien, Charles Williams, and Hugo Dyson met weekly at a tavern called the Eagle and Child in Oxford to discuss their work as well as to enjoy one another's company.

It's also helpful to avoid thinking of study as homework, otherwise we might give up even before starting. Instead, study is more like hunting for treasure. It is a tool that helps us dig deeper and deeper in the hopes of unearthing something valuable. We are digging with the expectation of finding something good, but we aren't sure exactly what. We are like the person in the parable from Matthew 13:44 who rejoices after discovering treasure hidden in a field and sells all he has to buy that field.

The exciting thing about this treasure hunt is that it never ends—the more we hunt, the better we get at hunting; and the better we get at hunting, the more treasure we discover. Treasure awaits for those who embark on the journey, but this quest also requires commitment to stay the course and not give up when it gets taxing. This is what it means to study as a spiritual practice.

BEGIN WITH A PRAYER AND THANKSGIVING

We know that the Lord is always ready to teach us, but it is also important that we approach study with an attitude of humility and openness to God's insight. As Isaiah says, God is the potter and we are the clay, and we must approach our studies with soft hearts that are teachable and moldable.

One way to reinforce this mind-set is to begin our time of study with a prayer, welcoming and inviting the Holy Spirit into the process. We welcome God's participation in the way we might invite an extraordinary pianist to collaborate with us to make beautiful music. We may not know how to play well, but the master pianist can gently guide us to something beautiful. As the writer of Proverbs says, "For the LORD gives wisdom; / from his mouth come knowledge and understanding" (Proverbs 2:6).

Study, when undertaken as a spiritual practice, takes place in a cooperative learning environment where the Holy Spirit has the role of facilitator, resource, guide, counselor, and mediator throughout our time. This enables us as participants to interact with God, to engage our questions, and to work toward our goal of knowing God better. As writer David Benner observed, "There is no deep knowing of God without a deep knowing of self and no deep knowing of self without a deep knowing of God."[6]

In Luke 11:13, Jesus says, "If you then, who are evil, know how to give good gifts to your children, how much more will the heavenly Father give the Holy Spirit to those who ask him!" God desires to give us the gift of interaction and learning, but we are not asking. If we ask, God will be with us and guide us through the Holy Spirit. In John 14:26, Jesus says, "But the Advocate, the Holy Spirit, whom the Father will send in my name, will teach you everything, and remind you of all that I have said to you."

In turn, we must show God our gratitude and give thanks for the opportunity to study who God is. This also should be a part of our prayer as we begin our time of study. In your prayers, expect God to hear you and thank God for the insight and knowledge you are about to receive. Better yet, come to this time with specific requests and expectations about what you want to learn and ask God to help.

In some ways, our time spent in study is like a family that took a long-awaited trip to Paris. Everyone was excited to go, especially the children, and the mom had prepared the kids by teaching them the basics of French language and culture. She told them all about the landmarks of Paris like the Arc de Triomphe, the Louvre, Notre Dame Cathedral, the palace at Versailles, and the Eiffel Tower.

The Eiffel Tower in particular caught the interests of the kids, and they couldn't wait to see it. As the plane approached Paris, the only thing the kids wanted to know was where the Eiffel Tower was. After searching for it from every angle in the plane, they finally spotted it. During the taxi ride to the hotel, they found it again. Once they settled in their room, they found it yet again. In fact, no matter where they went—a restaurant or a store or a museum—they wanted to know where it was, and they found it every time.

Why were the kids so successful at finding the Eiffel Tower? The simple answer is they were looking for it. The children were undeterred. They were determined to find it and would not give up until they did. Likewise, when we come to our studies looking for and expecting answers, we will find them. In Revelation 3:20, Jesus says, "Listen! I am standing at the door, knocking; if you hear my voice and open the door, I will come in to you and eat with you, and you with me." When we study, we must have our minds in the right place and expect an encounter with God.

THE BASICS AND THE CHALLENGES

On the last day of the school year, a first-grade teacher was touched to discover that her first graders had each given her a beautiful handwritten letter. She started to read each letter out loud, but as she read the heart-warming letters her emotions got the better of her and she began to choke up.

"I'm sorry," she said, "I'm having a hard time reading." One of her students spoke up, "It's okay. Just sound it out."

There are times when the nature of what we are studying can seem overwhelming; in those moments, we must return to the basics. When you study a passage, remember to prayerfully ask yourself:

- What is the takeaway from this passage?
- What is the passage emphasizing, reinforcing, or pointing out?
- Is there a particular message for me?

In Proverbs, the writer tells us: "Then I saw and considered it; / I looked and received instruction" (Proverbs 24:32). The spiritual practice of study gives us space to reflect, a moment to pause and consider what we are reading. It allows us to bypass the convenient understandings that are prepackaged for consumption and, by reflecting on the matter, wrestle with new ideas. This is at the root of engaging in study as a spiritual practice.

The practice of study can also force us to come face to face with some challenging realities. It's like the young man in high school whose friend became suddenly ill. It came on with no warning and worsened overnight, until the friend died the next morning. The young man was in complete disbelief over what had just unfolded. He remembered all the times they played basketball together in the park and the time spent at each other's houses reading comic books, playing in the backyard, and having dinner with their families. They were close, they had their whole lives ahead of them, and now his friend was gone.

When the day of the funeral came, school was dismissed so that students could attend the funeral, and the church was full. At the wake, the young man stood at the back of a long line that stretched outside the church. From the back of the church, he could see that there was an open casket. As the line slowly moved forward, he saw the outline of his friend's face from afar. This was the first dead person he had ever seen, and it gave him chills. The fact that it was someone he knew so well made it even tougher. It was all too real for him. Death, which had once seemed so mysterious and distant, now confronted him face to face. He was filled with unanswerable questions about the meaning of life and what it meant to live and die.

When we talk about study, we often think about it in a distant, antiseptic way, but we need to realize that examining these deep truths can also unsettle us and challenge us profoundly. When the disciples confronted the resurrected Christ, they were filled with questions and doubts. They were skeptical when the women told them that Jesus was, in fact, risen from the dead, and Thomas still doubted until he touched the scars in Jesus hands.

When we encounter God through study, we will have questions as well and they may well be just as profound. We bring these to God to investigate and examine alongside God and through the Holy Spirit. Wrestling with questions is hard, but it's why we study, because the wrestling of life's profound questions is more fulfilling than the unexamined faith.

BUT WHAT TO STUDY?

The question of what you should study is a deeply personal one. Is there a topic in your faith that you wish you could investigate further? Do you have a particular question or problem that's nagging at you? Study gives us the opportunity to investigate and examine these important questions. Without the practice of study, we might be left with only a superficial understanding of an issue based on little more than hearsay or cursory information. Study invites us to engage in the complexity of a topic.

When choosing what to study, here's a helpful rubric to figure out what you want to investigate and how to frame your process.

1. **Start with a question or problem**. This can really be anything. It may be a question you take from Scripture, or it could be something going on in society. The important thing is that it's something you don't know and want to learn.

2. **Determine the *why* question**. When asking the question, make sure that it's a why question and

not a who, what, when, or where question. A why question is about more than facts, it's a personal question that will motivate you to continue your study. Answering this question is the main goal of your study and the center of your investigation.

3. **Give yourself a time limit**. Tell yourself that you'll study a topic for a week or a month. The amount of time isn't important, but setting a time limit will help you avoid discouragement if you are feeling like your study will go on forever.

4. **Use logic**. John Wesley considered logic to be particularly important in understanding and interpreting Scripture, so much so that he ranked the knowledge of logic just below the knowledge of Scripture.[7]

5. **Spend time reflecting on your findings**. Once you've answered your question, take time to discern the implications of those answers and pray over the insights you've received. Ask God to help you find the relevance in your discoveries and how you can apply them to your life and your faith.

Using this framework, let's walk through a couple of examples. One question on the minds of many in the church has been the decline in church membership and attendance, especially since the 1970s. In the last few years, it has become well-known that the number of "nones," those who do not identify themselves with a religious affiliation, has spiked in the millennial generation. There is a lot of research that examines the reasons why these people have left the church.

However, one church study group decided to ask a very different question as they began to investigate the same phenomenon. Instead of asking why people were leaving the church, they asked themselves, "Why are young people staying in the church?"[8] After studying the issue, the group cited a number of reasons why millennials stay in church, but a few of the most important ones were connected to relational ties formed in church. These ties were with not only their peers but also a caring and welcoming community. Those who stayed also embraced outreach that made a strong impact in the community and engagement in meaningful theology and spiritual disciplines. One young adult commenting on the situation wrote, "We're not leaving the church because we don't find the cool factor there; we're leaving the church because we don't find Jesus there."

These are answers that the group found because they asked a why question, spent time to study the answer, used logic, and reflected on the implications of what they had discovered. When we study, we are like an investigator or a detective. What we find in our study are clues; with more and more study we are likely to find more clues. When we collect these clues in an organized way and make sense of them, we can find a common thread among the clues that help us start to form some kind of picture of what is really happening. As we add even more clues, we see the bigger picture come into sharper focus.

Let us take another topic that many churches need to study and understand: race.

Racial divisions in America run deep. While on first glance we may not think the Bible has a lot to offer on this subject, there are several passages that are directly relevant. For instance, Jesus used the parable of the Good Samaritan to speak directly to the racial rift between the Jews and the Samaritans.

In the ancient world, the Jews despised the Samaritans whom they considered a lesser race, though they shared a common ancestry. The Jews did not speak to the Samaritans and avoided walking through Samaria by traveling around it, even when it took them longer to do so.

Why the animosity? Samaria was originally part of Israel, but after the Assyrians conquered Samaria the new rulers resettled the land with foreigners who intermarried with the Israelites. Over time the Samaritans eventually became a racially distinct group. In addition, the Samaritans developed a rival religion that the Jews believed amounted to idolatry.

In Jesus' time, hatred of Samaritans was common among the Jewish people. By using a Samaritan as the central figure in his story about being a neighbor, Jesus challenged the people's racial bias.

"Who is my neighbor?" is a profound question, and Jesus' response had an enormous impact because the Lord had commanded the people to "Love the Lord your God with all your heart, and with all your soul, and with all your strength, and with all your mind; and your neighbor as yourself" (Luke 10:27). In asking his question, the lawyer was implying that it was okay to not love anyone whom he didn't consider his neighbor, but Jesus responded by saying that this theoretical non-neighbor did not exist.

In this parable, Jesus directly addressed the racially charged issues of his day. In response to the lawyer's question, Jesus made the despised Samaritan the undisputed champion of neighborliness and flipped his listeners' thinking upside down when he portrayed two pillars of Jewish society, a priest and a Levite, as the villains.

Another fascinating passage that broke racial taboos is Jesus' encounter with a Samaritan woman in John 4. When a Samaritan woman came to the well to draw water, Jesus asked her for a drink. Shocked that he would speak to her, the woman responded, "How is it that you, a Jew, ask a drink of me, a woman of Samaria?" (4:9) The passage goes on to unpack not only racial divisions but religious questions and questions of gender as well.

The point is that the spiritual practice of study is tailored to us and the questions that drive us, bother us, and intrigue us. Here is just a short list of sample topics that you or your group might dive into:

- Parenting
- Loneliness, depression, and anxiety
- Finances
- Pain and suffering
- Death and afterlife
- Salvation
- Spiritual realm and deliverance
- Church and its roles
- Human sexuality
- What does *community* mean?
- Race and ethnicity

Use the framework above and modify your study to your schedule and liking. If working together in a group, examine one topic at a time or assign a subtopic to each participant and ask each person to present his or her ideas to the rest of the group for discussion. No matter what you study, embrace this practice with the knowledge that the Holy Spirit is guiding you and that your study will bring you into a deeper and more knowledge of the God you serve.

STUDY

CENTER ON GOD

On February 4, 2018, a horrific collision took place in Cayce, South Carolina when a southbound Amtrak train heading to Miami collided with a CSX freight train. According to reports, the crash occurred because the train tracks were not lined up properly and the electrical signal system was out of service. Afterward, an engineer said, "Nobody could see what they're doing. It's called dark territory."

When we are not lined up properly, we can feel lost, confused or aimless, like we too are trains moving in dark territory. On Facebook and Instagram, we find others—perhaps our friends—who are wearing the latest fashions, who are eating at amazing restaurants, who are traveling to luxurious destinations, and we think that they must just have everything put together. They must just have better lives.

As a result, we are tempted to compare ourselves to others and forget that God tells each of us that we are "fearfully and wonderfully made" (Psalm 139:14). The discipline of study helps us align with God. It allows us a space where we can center ourselves and our relationship with our maker.

In his sermon, "The Importance and Advantage of a Thorough Knowledge of Divine Truth," Jonathan Edwards addresses how knowledge of divine things will help protect us from temptation. Edwards writes,

> For the devil often takes the advantage of persons' ignorance to ply them with temptations which otherwise would have no hold of them.
>
> By having much knowledge, you will be under greater advantages to conduct yourselves with prudence and discretion in your Christian course, and so to live much more to the honor of God and religion.[9]

TAKE NOTES

Many of us don't remember what we ate yesterday, let alone recall what we studied last week. Developing a system for taking notes helps to eliminate this problem. To take full advantage of the time we spend in study, it is important to develop a system for taking notes. Putting together the pieces of what we have learned in an organized system helps us better visualize what we study and connect the dots to see the full picture.

Let's say you want to study the way the word *love* is used and understood in the Bible. After a little bit of research into the way the word is used in the Greek New Testament, you'll discover that there are three words translated as *love*: *agape*, *phileo*, and *eros*. In your notes, you may want to break out each of these Greek words into its own section so you can see the way the three words function differently. This will allow the study of the word to produce better insights into the nature of love.

You may also want to take note of some of the questions you are bringing to your study. For instance, what are the distinctions between these different words? Which of the Greek words translated as "love" is used most often? Which writers use which versions of the word?

These questions will help direct your mind as you continue your study. For instance, in John 21:15-19, an interesting exchange between Peter and Jesus illustrates the difference between two of the words translated as "love" in English. This incident on the seashore was the third time Jesus appeared to the disciples after he was raised from the dead. Jesus eats breakfast with his disciples. After finishing the meal,

Jesus turns to Peter and asks, "Do you love me more than these?"

Peter replies, "Yes, Lord; you know that I love you." Jesus says, "Feed my lambs." In English, "love" is used in both the question and answer, but in the Greek the word Peter used for love was *phileo* while Jesus used *agape*.

Jesus asks Peter a second time, "Do you love [*agape*] me?"

Peter answers again, "Yes, Lord, you know that I love [*phileo*] you." Jesus says, "Tend my sheep."

Jesus then asks Peter a third time "Do you love me?" but this time Jesus does not use *agape* for love; he uses *phileo*.

Saddened that Jesus would ask a third time, Peter responds, "You know everything; you know that I love [*phileo*] you." To which Jesus again says, "Feed my sheep."

Passages like this give us some insight into how these different words are used. As we probe deeper into the meaning of the different words translated as "love" throughout the Bible, we will want to refer back to the discoveries made here. This can then affect the way we read the famous words from John 3:16, "For God so loved the world that gave his only Son, so that everyone who believes in him may not perish but may have eternal life" where the word *agape* is used.

In this example, we are left with questions like:

- What are the implications of this word choice?
- What does it mean that God loves?
- What do other passages say about love?

After some time spent in study, we can then return to our notes and review them. We may be surprised at some of the information we've collected and some of the revelations we have discovered.

Our notes can be a source of encouragement and clarification that enable us to discover wisdom that we did not previously have. We have started on this path of study because of a strong desire to meet God, and this desire only grows the more we learn. This desire will grow even stronger as you look back on where you have been and see how far you have come.

FINDING THE UNEXPECTED

The spiritual practice of study should never be viewed as homework, but instead as an enjoyable task. We are like explorers going off on an adventure. We don't know exactly what we will find, but we continue to search, nonetheless.

For one example, let's go back to the parable of the Good Samaritan. We all know the story of the Samaritan who helps the man who was beaten up on the side of the road, but a small detail that Jesus mentions often goes unremarked. Jesus says that the man applied wine and oil to the man's wounds and bandaged him.

To our modern ears, this raises an obvious question: why wine and oil?

When we dive further into the topic, we discover that wine acts as a disinfectant because it contains alcohol and would be helpful in cleansing the wound. Similarly, olive oil acts as a soothing lotion and complements the wine as a medicinal aid. *The International Standard Bible Encyclopedia* says: "Olive oil has certain curative qualities and is still used in modern medicine."[10] The mixture of the wine and oil acted as a disinfectant, which the Samaritan used to block infection and heal the wound.

This isn't necessarily the most important bit of information in this story, but it does teach us something unexpected. The spiritual practice of study isn't only about learning the answers to questions we are actively asking, but also about learning the things we never knew to ask.

STUDY WITH HUMILITY: SOLOMON

One morning, a teacher was driving to the high school where he taught when a police officer pulled him over. The officer walked over to the driver's window and, as he checked the driver's license and registration, several students from the high school began to drive past. Some honked their horns, while others laughed and pointed at their teacher. A few even yelled out to admonish their teacher for speeding.

Watching as all of this unfolded, the police officer returned to the driver and asked if he was a teacher at the school. The driver sheepishly replied that he was. At this, the officer smiled and said, "I think you've paid your debt to society today," and left without giving the teacher a ticket.

While we hope we don't need a story like this to learn it, the spiritual practice does require us to develop humility. If we think we know everything, then study probably won't be of much help. Instead, the practice of study starts from the premise that we need God for guidance and instruction.

With this in mind, we approach the practice of study with an openness to learn and even the assumption that we will have our prior beliefs challenged.

A terrific example of someone who had a humble desire to grow in knowledge and wisdom was Solomon. Solomon's ascension to the throne was not easy. Even before Solomon became king, two of

THE SURPRISING THINGS WE DID NOT KNOW

his older brothers had attempted to forcibly take the crown. Adonijah conspired to take the throne from David, and on another occasion, Absalom declared himself king and sparked a civil war between his followers and those loyal to his father, ultimately leading to Absalom's death.

Solomon must have learned from these failures, because after David died and Solomon ascended to the throne, God appeared to the twenty-year-old Solomon and asked, "Ask what I should give you." The young Solomon could have asked for anything—including the death of his enemies who were conspiring against him or a great military force to expand his kingdom—but that's not what Solomon asked for. Instead, Solomon humbly acknowledged his own ignorance and recognized that what he needed more than anything was wisdom and knowledge.

Solomon said, "Give me now wisdom and knowledge to go out and come in before this people, for who can rule this great people of yours" (2 Chronicles 1:10)?

Solomon's answer greatly pleased the Lord. God responded,

> Because this was in your heart, and you have not asked for possessions, wealth, honor, or the life of those who hate you, and have not even asked for long life, but have asked for wisdom and knowledge for yourself that you may rule my people over whom I have made you king, wisdom and knowledge are granted to you. I will also give you riches, possessions, and honor, such as none of the kings had who were before you, and none after you shall have the like. (2 Chronicles 1:11-12)

Like Solomon, we must approach our study of Scripture with humility and a heart that wants to know

God. In return, God will honor our request and guide us in our work.

STUDY TO EXPERIENCE GOD

As the man entered the court room, he could not stop thinking about what a horrible mistake he had made. He had been caught driving under the influence. Again. It was only two weeks after his first arrest, and, as he entered the courtroom for the second time, he was dismayed to see that the judge was the same one who had presided over his first arrest. The judge recognized him instantly and barked at him, "I told you to get help and to never appear in my courtroom ever again!"

It was the worst day of the man's life. He knew it went against his better judgment to drive while drunk. He thought about the impending sentence and what it would do his family, especially to his children. It was his fault—and he knew it. He couldn't pass it off or make some excuse. He screwed up. He had brought all this trouble on himself

Then, in this moment of despair, something amazing happened. The judge told the man he would personally volunteer to sponsor the man in Alcoholics Anonymous (AA) and would use his influence as a judge to get the man into an outpatient rehab center.

The man could not believe what had just happened. He was obviously overjoyed, but also wondered what had possessed the judge to do this? When asked, the judge responded, "I heard a sermon in my church about God's mercy and grace and it led me to help you."

The judge's knowledge of God's mercy and grace was not mere academic knowledge. It was not a lifeless series of facts, dates, and rote memorization. This knowledge of God's mercy was alive, and it touched the judge's soul and moved him to offer mercy to someone who didn't deserve it. People would have applauded the judge if he had ruled harshly and thrown the book at the man, but he did the unusual thing because the knowledge of God lived in him and manifested through him.

If we look at study the way we have in the past, then we will miss the point. Instead, the spiritual practice of study leads us to a knowledge of God that is "living and active" (Hebrews 4:12). By practicing mercy and grace, the judge experienced God and manifested God to this man.

The man's heart was touched, but no one could not have foreseen what happened next. God moved the man's heart, and after a few years he became a pastor. Since then he has been sober for over forty years and he has sponsored many others in Alcoholics Anonymous, has spoken publicly against drinking at public schools, and has led many others to Christ.

The knowledge of God changed a judge's heart, and in turn, he changed another man's life who, in turn, changed the lives of so many others. We don't know what verse the preacher used on that Sunday when the judge sat in the pews, but perhaps the judge heard Philippians 2:1-4:

> If then there is any encouragement in Christ, any consolation from love, any sharing in the Spirit, any compassion and sympathy, make my joy complete: be of the same mind, having the same love, being in full accord and of one mind. Do nothing from selfish ambition or conceit, but in humility regard others as better than yourselves. Let each of you look not to your own interests, but to the interests of others.

During an interview, a renowned music producer was asked how he knew if a potential artist had the "it" factor necessary for success. The producer's answer was short and sweet. "It moves me," he said and elaborated that he knew when the music touched his heart and filled his soul.

Study has the same capacity to allow us to experience God and let God touch our hearts and fill our souls. Too many see Christianity as a lifeless religion that has no power. For some, Christianity is reduced to little more than rules and rituals. But when we study as a spiritual practice, we open ourselves to experience Christ.

Our mission is not to study a dead person in the history books, but rather to study someone risen from the dead and to partake in his resurrection. As Paul declared, "I want to know Christ" (Philippians 3:10). For Paul and for us, Christ is alive.

Study has the ability to bring the biblical narrative to life and enables us to experience God in new ways. Take for example the shortest verse in the Bible, John 11:35, which says "Jesus wept." Jesus' heart was touched, and he was moved to tears when Lazarus died. As Jesus approached Lazarus' village, he witnessed the great sorrow and pain of those close to Lazarus.

Our practice of study challenges us to ask, not only what is happening in this story, but also how we can understand Jesus' heart, how to feel what he felt, and what it means to be in pain like Jesus was in pain.

Today, tourists can visit Jerusalem and spend time in the places where Jesus spent time. They can visit the Garden Tomb, for instance, which many believe to be the actual tomb of Jesus. The Garden Tomb stands next to Gordon's Calvary, the spot where the formation of rocks resembles the shape of a skull. Many say that was where Jesus was crucified.

As you approach the tomb, you will notice a trench was dug in front of the opening for the massive stone that once covered the entryway. The opening of the tomb is very small, and you have to bend and duck in order to enter. Millions of visitors have made their way to see this empty tomb.

Being in this place, we can imagine the disbelief of the women in Luke 24 as they first noticed that the massive stone had been moved away and that Jesus was no longer there. We can imagine Peter running to see for himself, stooping and looking in to discover that the women were telling the truth.

The spiritual practice of study helps us experience God and, therefore, helps us walk with God. Using our imagination allows us to visit places, such as the cold stone chamber of the tomb. It helps us feel the way Jesus' followers felt when they realized that he was not there but had risen.

STUDY TAKES FOCUS AWAY FROM OURSELVES

In his letter to the Philippians, Paul wrote, "I, too, have reason for confidence in the flesh" (3:4). In simpler terms, Paul is saying that he has a lot of things he could boast about. In the following verses, Paul lists his prestigious titles and privileges and the respect people pay him.

Paul doesn't do this to boast about himself, but is responding to others, whom he calls "dogs" and "evil workers" (v. 2) who have been misleading believers by brandishing their credentials. To make an analogy to contemporary times, Paul would admonish Christians today who use titles, degrees, and positions of power to dominate the faithful. In contrast to this reliance on self, Paul urges the believers to the "excellence of the knowledge of Christ" (v. 8, NKJV™). In comparison, Paul regarded all of the worldly gains, titles and acknowledgments as "rubbish" and "as loss" because of Christ (v. 7-8, NRSV).

What would make Paul say all these things? He answers in Philippians 3:10 when he declares, "I want to know Christ."

The spiritual practice of study bends the spotlight away from us and turns it toward Christ. The more we know Christ, the more we want to, as Paul wrote, "[become] like him" (v. 10).

Paul's intense desire to know Christ stems from his knowledge of Christ's death and resurrection. To truly know about God's work of salvation, we, like Paul, need to come to grips with the gravity of our sins and the amazing love of Christ that has been offered to us. To know Christ and his redemptive work in our lives is to experience salvation.

STUDYING IS SEARCHING

In our studies, there will be questions. Some of them will be answered and some will not. In fact, in pursuit of answers to our questions we may frustratingly produce even more questions. That may sound annoying, but we should not be discouraged or lose hope.

Jesus answered many questions during his ministry, but sometimes he answered questions with a question of his own. For example, after Jesus had the audacity to heal a man on the sabbath, his accusers asked, "Is it lawful to cure on the sabbath?" Jesus responded, "Suppose one of you has only one sheep and it falls into a pit on the sabbath; will you not lay hold of it and lift it out" (Matthew 12:10-11)?

His accusers were thinking and responding in one way, but Jesus flipped their thinking on its head and challenged them to think about the question from a different perspective. They did not get the answer they were looking for, or really a concrete answer at all, but, if they were listening, they received a terrific insight into God's heart.

After Adam and Eve sinned, the first thing God does is ask a question: "Where are you? (Genesis 3:9)" God asked, "Where are you?" because Adam and Eve went into hiding after eating from the fruit. Of course, God knew they were hiding, but God wanted them to think about their situation and be truthful when they answered.

Study can frustrating at times and exciting at others, but it will always be personal. In fact, the spiritual practice of study can be intimidating because it promises to challenge us, even to our core. Nevertheless, we should continue to pursue study with openness and anticipation of these challenges; through these challenges, we will be invited to engage with God.

If we honestly answer the question, "Where are you?" that God asked in the garden, we become bare before God. We expose our weaknesses and failures. Only then can we have an authentic conversation with God. Our struggle with meaningful questions enriches our faith and journey.

God always wants us to go deeper in our understanding and knowledge. As the psalmist cries out:

> O God, you are my God, I seek you,
> my soul thirsts for you;
> my flesh yearns for you;
> as in a dry and weary land where there is
> no water. (Psalm 63:1)

God delights in those who search after God. Deuteronomy 4:29 tells us that we will find God "if you search after him with all your heart and soul."

Think of study as a tool to help us to search for and seek after God. The process of searching strengthens the foundations of our faith and enables us to add new layers of understanding.

BE TEACHABLE

An NFL coach was asked in an interview to describe what separates a good player from a great one. His answer wasn't superior talent or extraordinary physical skills or unmatched determination. Instead, the coach said that a great player wants to be taught, wants to be motivated, and wants to be inspired. It's a simple yet revealing indicator of greatness, and it's so obvious that many overlook it. Given its simplicity, one may wonder why many overlook it, but the straightforwardness of the idea belies its elusiveness.

Everyone has heard about the importance of being taught, motivated, and inspired since we were little. Teachers, coaches, speakers, and preachers drill these ideas into us. Because they are so widely accepted as basic ingredients to success, it seems as if we have tuned out their full meaning.

The key words in the coach's answer are actually the words "wants to." Someone may ask, "Doesn't everyone want to?" Especially football players, who've reached the highest level of their profession, wouldn't they want to be taught, motivated, and inspired?

Unfortunately, the answer is no. Some may think that they have achieved enough and no longer need teaching or motivation or inspiration, but the great players know that in order to remain great, this drive can never diminish. The great ones know that if they stop learning and pushing, they will go backward.

Football fans see the game on Sunday, which lasts maybe three hours. What they don't see are the hours upon hours of studying, preparation, and meetings that take place in anticipation of the game. Months and months are spent learning and mentally preparing for those three hours. Dick Vermeil, a Super Bowl winning coach, said, "You show [the playbook] to an everyday person . . . and they can't get over it. They just couldn't envision what was going into NFL preparation."[11]

Just as poor or excellent preparation will result in a different result on game-day, our preparation will make a similar difference in our faith. Study is an under-appreciated spiritual practice among Christians today. An NFL player does not stop learning once he reaches a level of greatness, and a Christian should not stop learning once he or she has reached a certain level of spiritual maturity. Instead we should keep pushing and striving, refining our skills, passing them on, and perfecting them over time.

Questions for Personal Reflection and Group Discussion

1. How do you respond to Paul's analogy about solid food and spiritual maturity? Why is it important for us to build up to more complex and difficult topics of study? What benefits does it give us when we finally reach these meatier topics?

2. Walk through the five steps about what to study that are listed in this chapter. What do you want to study with your group? When will you study? What questions do you want to answer?

3. Why is it important for us to come to our studies with humility? How does the example of Solomon speak to how we should prepare for our time in study?

4. What does it mean to be *teachable*? How can we set our minds in a way that God can teach us and help us learn?

CHAPTER 3
Growing Closer to God

OPENING PRAYER

> If you accept my words
> > and treasure up my commandments within you,
> making your ear attentive to wisdom,
> > and inclining your heart to understanding;
> if you indeed cry out for insight,
> > and raise your voice for understanding;
> if you seek it like silver,
> > and search for it as for hidden treasures—
> then you will understand the fear of the LORD
> > and find the knowledge of God.
> For the LORD gives wisdom;
> > from his mouth come knowledge and
> > > understanding. (Proverbs 2:1-6)

THE POWER SOURCE

Recently, I was waiting in a doctor's office flipping through the magazines they had displayed when I saw an advertisement for a new SUV. The design was sleek and inviting, and as I read the ad more closely, a number of interesting features caught my eye. For one, the car had wireless smartphone charging capabilities; it can recharge your phone all by itself while it's just sitting there. In addition, the car came with electrical outlets and USB ports in all three rows.

Who knew we needed so many electrical outlets and ports? When I was growing up, we still had to roll down our car windows by hand. Nowadays, a plethora of new electronic devices routinely fight for our attention no matter where we are. It's a good bet that your family has plenty of them, and as a result, a power source and a place to recharge has become a top priority.

For many of us, the thought of being without power and without a cell phone sets off a minor panic attack. Perhaps someday someone will invent a battery that never goes dead, but until that happens, we will have to recharge them regularly to get them to work.

We have all experienced "low battery" moments, not just with our technology, but in our emotional and spiritual lives as well. These are the times when we are at our wits end and our souls feel out of sync. These are the days when we feel exhausted and over-whelmed. We all feel like the person who said, "I'm retired: I was tired yesterday and I'm still tired today." We all need a break, a refresher, and a safe haven in which we can reenergize from the demands of our lives.

It would be wonderful if we could park ourselves in a charging station and recharge our batteries like we do with our cell phones, but how do we do that with our souls? How do we recover meaning when we lose the thread? How do we recover our purpose?

In Ezekiel 37:11, the people of Israel are depicted as a valley full of dried bones that say, "Our bones are dried up, and our hope is lost." Yet despite being in this barren and lifeless condition, God breathes life back into them. God says, "I will put my spirit within you, and you shall live, and I will place you on your own soil; then you shall know that I, the Lord, have spoken and will act, says the Lord" (Ezekiel 37:14).

Think about that for a moment. God is promising nothing less than a resurrection. When we study God's promises and begin to understand the experiences others have had with God, we are rejuvenated. Practicing study as a spiritual discipline allows us to draw from the "living water" Jesus talks about in the Gospel of John. The more we listen and drink in God's story, the more we appreciate and understand what Scripture is trying to share with us. This allows us to absorb the many layers of meaning in the Bible and acquire a deeper understanding of God.

Let's look at Psalm 42 for an example. The psalm opens, "As the deer pants for streams of water, / so my soul pants for you, my God" (Psalm 42:1, NIV). Focus on the verb "pants." It is a very descriptive and visual word. You can almost hear what's happening. If you have dogs, you have seen them pant after jumping around in the backyard or after a long run.

Panting describes a kind of desperate thirst, so desperate that you cannot stop. You are out of air and struggling to breathe. At that stage, the only thing that matters is where you can find water. If you have seen a dog once it has found water, you have seen them relish it as if it's the best tasting water they have ever had. This is the way our souls pant after God. Think about what happens when our souls finally find what they are longing for.

REAL ENCOUNTER WITH GOD

People today have a thirst and hunger for connection, whether it's a connection to people or a connection to God. Yet, at the same time, we also have a deep-seated sense of mistrust. From an early age, we teach our kids about "stranger danger." While it's valuable to teach children to protect themselves, too often these walls continue to stifle us long into adulthood.

When we pair this mistrust with the unintended consequences of our modern world, we create a potent cocktail that prevents us from having real encounters with others. Take social media for instance. Many people who use social media feel a sense of anonymity and thus feel free to vent in ways they would normally avoid if they were speaking to someone face to face. This leads them to hurt others and speak harshly. In "connecting" ourselves online we have become increasingly disconnected from one another in reality.

Only in face-to-face communication can we experience the humanity of another person. We can sympathize with a friend who shares about their pain on Facebook, but it is another thing entirely to sit with that person one on one, look them in the eyes, and see the image of God looking back. When we do that, we don't just connect with the idea of them but with the very essence of who they are. We empathize with them, and we begin to become a community.

When we see a human face, we feel connected to them and feel a sense of responsibility to help. Online friendships certainly have their place, but they also have their limitations. Our capacity to experience the humanity in ourselves and in others is increasingly minimalized as we substitute technological advancement for human connection.

These distant and disconnected relationships in some ways symbolize the relationship many of us have with God. We appreciate the idea of God, but the actual intimate personal interaction is missing. The spiritual practice of study empowers us to have a face-to-face encounter with God. Study provides us with the opportunity to spend time with God. When we do that, we can begin to identify with the psalmist who says,

> My soul longs, indeed it faints
> for the courts of the LORD;
> my heart and my flesh sing for joy
> to the living God. (Psalm 84:2)

When we come face-to-face with the Almighty, we "taste and see" the goodness of the Lord. As Psalm 84:10 declares about God, "A day in your courts is better / than a thousand elsewhere."

GROW IN FAITH AND STUDY

Good friends are precious. Good friends can sense when something is wrong with us in an instant because they know us to our very core. Even when we try to cover it up, they know. When embarrassing things have happened to you, a good friend is still there. We all cherish good friends, but we also realize that these friendships don't happen immediately when you first meet someone. They have to grow and develop over time. When we invest in these friendships, our lives get brighter as a result.

The same is true of our relationship with Jesus. You may have first been introduced to Jesus as a child or a teenager; maybe you've known Jesus our entire life. Alternatively, maybe you met Jesus as an adult at one of the forks in life's road where you realize that you need Jesus' redemptive presence. It may have been dramatic, and it may have been routine, but one thing is certain, you know Jesus personally and he knows you.

Over time, this relationship with Jesus has developed just like a relationship with a good friend. The spiritual practice of study is just one more way to get to know this friend better and to strengthen your relationship. Knowledge of Christ is not like the knowledge you gain while reading a biography, it's more like the intimate insight we gain from being with our friend through all the ups and downs of life.

We allow good friends to get close to us, and in turn, we are invited into a privileged space alongside our friends. As part of this closeness, we can count on them to give us their honest, unvarnished feedback.

As we experience Christ in our studies, we open our hearts to him and allow Christ to guide and counsel us. We trust our good friends because we believe that they have our best interests in mind, and we love them for that. In the same way, Jesus has our best interests in mind. When we study, we interact with Christ and we learn his ways.

STUDY FILLS US WITH GOD'S WORDS

One day, a junior-high teacher was having a particularly difficult time with her students. No matter what she did, they would not stop fighting during class and making fun of each other. Eventually, she stopped her lesson and told them to put away their books and to take out a blank sheet of paper. She instructed them to list the names of their classmates on the left-hand side of the page. On the right-hand side, she told them to write the nicest thing they could think of about that person.

Although the exercise was intended to calm the class down and bring them back to the lesson plan, after reading them to herself, the teacher decided that the kind words needed to be heard. Over the weekend, the teacher wrote the name of each student on a separate sheet and below their names she copied what others said about them.

When she handed out the sheets with their names, the students were taken aback. One of the first students responded, "Wow! Really?" while another shared, "I never knew that meant anything to anyone!" The teacher was delighted to see the excited responses from the students, but she didn't think much of it until years later when she attended a funeral for one of her former students.

After the funeral service, the parents of the young man who died approached the teacher and said, "We want to show you something. This was what he was carrying when he was killed." The father pulled out a piece of paper and the teacher immediately recognized her own handwriting. It was the list that she painstakingly copied down for each student.

She was moved by what the boy's parents shared, but that was not the end of it. Other former students who listened to the conversation started to chime in. One student said he kept his list in his desk at home. Another said she placed the cherished list in her wedding album. A third student proudly pulled out his wallet and there it was, folded and tucked away among his prized possessions. The teacher was overwhelmed and started to cry. How could a simple assignment designed to pull their attention back to the lesson make such a huge and lasting impact?

While this is an uplifting story, it also illustrates the emotional-drought conditions that many of us live in. Our society is used to cutting others down. We have become so conditioned to do this to one another that people are starved for encouraging and uplifting words.

The spiritual practice of study serves as a kind of medication for this disease. We are giving ourselves generous doses of affirming and encouraging words from God. It doesn't cost us anything to study, but the rewards are priceless. When we are reminded of our God-given value, it changes the way we look at ourselves. The students in this teacher's class understood instinctively that they needed to keep those words close by, otherwise they might forget the beautiful and heart-warming things others said about them.

Study keeps God's words close to us. We hold and remember God's beautiful words, and we turn to them to remind us who we are and what God has said about us. A famous preacher once wrote that the Bible is like God's love letter to us; God writes to us to tell us, not only that God loves us, but what God has done out of love and affection for us. In the process of studying, we are depositing good, positive, and uplifting words to our spiritual banks.

Through study, we examine and reflect life-giving words that transform the understanding of our worth. When the issue of an individual's worth came up, Jesus asked his followers, "Which one of you, having a hundred sheep and losing one of them, does not leave the ninety-nine in the wilderness and go after the one that is lost until he finds it" (Luke 15:4)? The idea that God loves some people less was so preposterous that Jesus made the point that he would leave ninety-nine in the wilderness to find the one lost sheep.

At the same time, we can experience spiritual bankruptcy when too many words of disappointment, guilt, and failure are deposited into our banks. The lack of life-giving words is so far-reaching that John Gottman, a researcher, was able to predict the success rate of marriages based on the ratio of positive to negative experiences (words and emotions). Gottman argued that a balance between positive and negative experiences must be reached in order for a marriage to succeed. However, Gottman discovered that five positives were necessary to cancel out one negative. If negative experiences outweighed the positive, Gottman predicted marital failure. Out of the 700 married couples that he interviewed and studied, Gottman's theory was correct 94 percent of the time.[1]

The spiritual practice of study reminds us of God; God's good words will be written on our hearts. What we have written down on our hearts will determine the story of our lives. We want God's words to live in us and to shape our thinking and to guide our decision-making.

Think about it in the opposite way. Without God's words, what kind of words will be written on our hearts? Words are like seeds, and when negative words consume us, they produce their own kind of fruit. When negative feelings or thoughts dwell in our hearts, we will bear the fruits of frustration, anger, and despair.

These negative thoughts and emotions can act as toxins to our souls. Sometimes we need to purge them for our own benefit. The study of God's refreshing words will cleanse our souls of these negative thoughts and spiritual toxins that have accumulated inside of us.

Studying the redemptive power of Christ can be like a soothing balm over our inner wounds. The classic spiritual, "There Is a Balm in Gilead" declares:

> Sometimes I feel discouraged,
>   and think my work's in vain,
> but then the Holy Spirit
>   revives my soul again.

STUDY

> There is a balm in Gilead
> to make the wounded whole;
> There is a balm in Gilead
> to heal the sin-sick soul.
>
> Don't ever feel discouraged,
> for Jesus is your friend,
> and if you look for knowledge
> he'll ne'er refuse to lend.[2]

As the hymn tells us, if we look to Jesus "for knowledge," he "ne'er refuse to lend." The knowledge of Christ will help us through the tough times.

Some people may go through life wearing a label that others have placed upon them. When we study what God thinks of us, it is like finding a divine eraser that can cleanse those words from the tablet of our hearts and erase those feelings of paralyzing guilt.

Study allows us to focus on God's promises and not on these negative thoughts. We can expel the hurtful words with God's words. Study will help us to write a new chapter in our lives with words that declare what God thinks of us. Read God's promise in Isaiah 43:1-7:

> But now thus says the LORD,
> he who created you, O Jacob,
> he who formed you, O Israel:
> Do not fear, for I have redeemed you;
> I have called you by name, you are mine.
> When you pass through the waters, I will be
> with you;
> and through the rivers, they shall not
> overwhelm you;
> when you walk through fire you shall not be
> burned,

and the flame shall not consume you.
For I am the Lord your God,
the Holy One of Israel, your Savior.
I give Egypt as your ransom,
Ethiopia and Seba in exchange for you.
Because you are precious in my sight,
and honored, and I love you,
I give people in return for you,
nations in exchange for your life.
Do not fear, for I am with you;
I will bring your offspring from the east,
and from the west I will gather you;
I will say to the north, "Give them up,"
and to the south, "Do not withhold;
bring my sons from far away
and my daughters from the end of the earth—
everyone who is called by my name,
whom I created for my glory,
whom I formed and made.

STUDY THE HEART OF GOD

The Bible is filled with instances in which God interacts with people and how these interactions reveal God's heart and priorities. For instance, God gave a very interesting law to the Israelites in Leviticus 23:22, "When you reap the harvest of your land, you shall not reap the very edges of your field, or gather the gleanings of your harvest; you shall leave them for the poor and for the alien: I am the Lord your God." Following God's command, the people would leave all of the edges of their fields unharvested. In addition, after harvesting their grain, the people were instructed not to go back to the field to collect what they missed the first time around. The crops on the edge of the fields and what was left behind were for the poor.

STUDY

God's rationale for this was simple. The people needed to share. It's a kind of generosity we find throughout Scripture as we're told to be generous to the poor, the strangers, and the foreigners.

But it is much more than that. By leaving the corners of the edges unattended and leaving grain on the fields, we invite foreigners and the poor to partake of our harvest. We are welcoming them to our property.

There is another side to this commandment as well. The system is set up so that the people are helping to feed the foreigners and the poor, but they are not directly feeding them. Instead, God arranges a situation where the foreigners and the poor collect the grains themselves. On one hand, this helps preserve the dignity of those gleaning the fields. They do not have to beg or ask for a handout. On the other hand, by extending their generosity to foreigners and the poor, the landowners get to interact with the poorest in their community.

In America today, the income disparity between the rich and poor has never been so wide. The wealthy can choose to avoid interacting with the poorest people by moving into gated communities and exclusive neighborhoods. One wonders if they are missing out by secluding themselves.

In the arrangement that God designed, the landowners interacted with foreigners, strangers, and the poor. They saw one another face-to-face, and sometimes, they even married each other. Ruth was a Moabite, in other words, a foreigner who "gleaned in the field behind the reapers" of the fields owned by Boaz, "a prominent rich man" in Bethlehem (Ruth 2:1,3). Boaz observed the law about not gleaning after the harvest, thus enabling Ruth to follow the reapers and collect the leftovers.

After Boaz learned of Ruth's outstanding character and backstory with Naomi, her mother-in-law, Boaz told Ruth, "Now listen, my daughter, do not go to glean in another field or leave this one, but keep close to my young women. Keep your eyes on the field that is being reaped, and follow behind them. I have ordered the young men not to bother you. If you get thirsty, go to the vessel and drink from what the young men have drawn" (Ruth 2:8-9). Eventually, Boaz married Ruth and they had a son, Obed, who was the father of David, who would become the greatest king in Israel's history.

God's concern for foreigners, strangers, and the oppressed and disenfranchised is highlighted throughout the Bible. Deuteronomy 10:19 tells us "You shall also love the stranger, for you were strangers in the land of Egypt." According to Psalm 146:9, "The LORD watches over the strangers; / he upholds the orphan and the widow." In the parable of sheep and goats, the king welcomed and praised those who gave food to the hungry, gave drink to the thirsty, and welcomed the stranger (Matthew 25:35).

All of these stories teach us about God's heart and what it means to search after God. All of them are revealed to us in more depth when we embrace the practice of study.

STUDY MAKES KNOWLEDGE OF GOD A FOUNDATION

Eight-year-old Sandy had been anxiously waiting for four weeks to go fishing with Grandpa. In preparation for the trip, Sandy dug up worms for bait and got her gear ready. When the day finally came, it rained— not just ordinary rain, but pouring rain.

Sandy was furious and began stamping her feet around the house while angrily staring out of the

STUDY

window. "Why couldn't God let it rain yesterday!" Sandy cried out.

Grandpa tried to explain to Sandy how beneficial the rain was, but she was having none of it. Surprisingly, the rain stopped around two o'clock, giving Sandy and her grandpa just enough time to go out to the lake.

They quickly loaded up the car with their gear and headed out. When they got out on the lake, Sandy was amazed. Because of the rainstorm, the fish were really biting. They caught more fish that day than they ever had, more than enough for everyone back home.

At the family's fish dinner that night, Sandy was asked to say grace. She concluded her prayer by saying, "And, Lord, if I sounded grumpy earlier today, it was because I didn't know."

If Sandy knew, she would not have been anxious and upset. In fact, if she knew, she would have been excited that it rained since it made for a better day of fishing! What a difference knowing makes.

The spiritual practice of study keeps us grounded and anchors our knowledge of God to the center of our Christian experience. This offers us a strong foundation when waves of uncertainty come our way. The knowledge of God provides roots to our faith like the wise man who built his house on rock by applying God's words (Matthew 7:24-25).

Emotions provide thrills and excitement, but they are not a sound guide. Paul wrote about some members of the faithful, "I can testify that they have a zeal for God, but it is not enlightened" (Romans 10:2). The King James Version says their zeal for God is "not according to knowledge." The Greek word that Paul used is *epignosis*, which can be defined as "to become thoroughly acquainted with, to know thoroughly; to know accurately, know well."

While zeal for God is important, it needs to rest on divine knowledge, otherwise it can lead believers to drift without an anchor. Paul continued, "For, being ignorant of righteousness that comes from God, and seeking to establish their own, they have not submitted to God's righteousness" (Romans 10:3). In other words, the lack of knowledge made them ignorant of the true righteousness, and as such, they could not believe or submit to God's righteousness. They ended up making up their own ideas of righteousness.

What Paul observed in the first century has not changed much. Today, many live for the immediate experience or for the moment. In some Christian circles, the appeal of an emotional worship experience is tantalizing. Fun has become an important social currency; missing out on fun brings anxiety and despair. If people expect their Christian experience to be based on emotion, the risk of putting our subjective experience above the knowledge of God clouds the beautiful picture God wants us to see of ourselves and our world.

ROOTLESSNESS

Sociologists are talking about the rootlessness of American society. More people today are moving to different states and different parts of the country than ever before. There is nothing wrong with this; people are free to live wherever they wish, but one consequence of the relocation of people across the country is that they don't feel deeply connected to the new area that they move into. They don't have roots in the area.

In sociological studies, people who have moved around to different places feel less responsibility to the area. This is not because they are not civic minded, not because they don't care, and not because they are irresponsible. Instead, it's because they feel less connected to the local issues and local context. This disconnection has an impact on our civic duties as well. In 2000, a study in the *American Journal of Political Science* reported that people who had stayed in one place for at least three years voted at a rate nearly 11 percentage points higher than those had moved within a year of election day.

A researcher wrote, "When people move to a new area, they don't know who's on the school board or who their state senator is. They don't know the new policies of their location. They have to learn about the local issues—while at the same time getting adjusted to their new homes and schools for their kids."[3]

STUDY GIVES ROOTS

The world's largest living things are the Sequoia trees in California's Sierra Nevada mountains. They also happen to be the world's tallest trees. The largest Sequoia has a width of 35 feet. Some of them are so wide that cars are able to drive through tunnels carved out at the base of the tree. The tallest Sequoia stands 367 feet, which is taller than the Statue of Liberty.

You will be even more amazed to learn about the conditions in which these "super trees" grow. First, the region gets hardly any rain and regularly experiences long droughts. In the Sierra Nevada mountains, it's cold year-round and the typical growing season only lasts 6-9 weeks. Temperatures are cool even during the growing season and frost can occur 12 months of the year. The Sierra Nevada region is also known for violent winds. There is hardly any vegetation because the winds physically batter the plants, lashing everything in sight with snow and ice. But it gets even worse! Because it's a mountainous region the soil is thin, coarse, and nutrient-poor. The violent winds constantly erode away soil.

So, how do these trees grow? How do they overcome the harshest conditions in order to become the greatest trees? Because they have little soil, Sequoias grow their roots right below the surface of the ground. Then, these magnificent trees inter-lock their roots together underground. They stand together and hold each other up when violent winds come. They cannot survive on their own. They are stronger because they are locked-in with each other.[4]

The spiritual practice of study helps us to grow roots. As our roots keep growing, they connect with God, and we become rooted with God.

As a contrasting example to the Sequoia trees, consider trees that have been grown in biospheres, which are enclosed bubbles that look like giant greenhouses. These trees grow up with the best of everything: plenty of sunshine, water, soil, and extra nutrients.

You may think these trees have the best chances of becoming the strongest trees, but that is hardly the case. When these trees are replanted in the real environment, they can't make it. When conditions are sunny and mild, they're fine, but when harsh weather comes and fierce winds blow, they slowly wither away.

Their "perfect" environment did not prepare them for harsh conditions. Their roots were adequate to hold them up in normal conditions but not in difficult ones. Study enriches our faith by extending our roots deeper into the knowledge of God that not only opens our world to God's perspective but also anchors and secures our lives in divine knowledge

STUDY FULFILLS OUR DESIRE TO KNOW

Study helps to satisfy one of our deepest longings. At some level, every civilization understands humanity's desire to know. The motto for TV's *Star Trek* is to venture forth into "the final frontier" and "to boldly go where no man has gone before." The fundamental promise of science is new discoveries and new technologies, or, in simpler terms, new knowledge.

We want to know, and the spiritual practice of study helps us know more. In every industry, business, government, and educational system, there are consultants. Consulting groups, some with global connections, are in high demand because they provide expert advice in a given field. Study is like seeking consultation with God.

Like the psalmist, we seek answers to our deepest questions:

> Make me to know your ways, O Lord;
>   teach me your paths.
> Lead me in your truth, and teach me,
>   for you are the God of my salvation;
>   for you I wait all day long. (Psalm 25:4-5)

God invites those who seek God to approach and ask. Proverbs 8:17 states, "I love those who love me, / and those who seek me diligently find me." God, according to Paul, "has shone in our hearts to give the light of the knowledge of the glory of God in the face of Jesus Christ" (2 Corinthians 4:6).

Augustine wrote, "You have made us for yourself, O Lord, and our hearts are restless until they rest in you (*Confessions* I, 1:1)." In *Mere Christianity*, C.S. Lewis declared, "If I find in myself a desire which no experience in this world can satisfy, the most probable explanation is that I was made for another world."[5] Blaise Pascal, the 17th-century French philosopher spoke of the "infinite abyss" in the hearts of people that "can be filled only with an infinite and immutable object; in other words by God himself."[6]

DIGGING FOR GOLD

We have been hard wired to know God. Knowing God fills an empty room in our hearts. Study enables us to know God more.

Studying is like mining below the surface to seek some kind of prized ore, like gold or silver. Our hard work and effort are occasionally rewarded with golden nuggets of knowledge, insight, and beauty. It is through these that God touches our hearts, minds, and souls.

In our first attempts at digging, we should not get discouraged if our efforts do not yield something right away. The act of digging is an important part of the process. Digging is work, but we are trying to get deeper and deeper below the surface.

The act of digging enables us to learn and to be awake. It allows us to open up to God. God is with us in the mining journey.

DISCOVERING OURSELVES THROUGH STUDY

After a long morning, two construction work-ers paused midday for their lunch break. As they opened up their lunch pails, one of them cried out as he looked inside his box: "Not bologna again! I can't believe it. I hate bologna! This is the third time this week I've had bologna! I can't stand baloney!"

His buddy sitting next to him asked, "Why don't you just ask your wife to make you something different?" He replied, "I don't have a wife. I made these myself."

For some reason, we keep feeding ourselves bologna when we don't like it. Sometimes we don't know why we keep doing the things we do. Paul expressed the same sentiment in Romans 7:15, "I do not understand my own actions. For I do not do what I want, but I do the very thing I hate." Study gives clarity to our spiritual learning and growth in a way that few others can. Study is neither blind nor unthinking.

We must make sure to remind ourselves that we have a personal stake in this. We are learning to draw closer to God. Remembering our purpose brings with it the motivation that enhances our level of commitment. Because learning is personal, we are challenged to weigh perspectives that we might not have considered before. When we test ourselves physically and mentally, we grow because we push our limits. Physically, we get stronger. Mentally, our learning becomes enriched. In a similar way, when we study we push ourselves to grow, expand, and strengthen in faith.

When we are challenged, expect surprises. At the outset, no one would have thought Ashley would go far with her studies. She came from a lower-income background and her parents suffered from drug addiction. Even though she was in high school, Ashley became like a parent figure to her younger siblings.

In spite of all her challenges, she achieved a near-perfect score on the SAT and graduated as the salutatorian of her high-school class.

Her story was simply remarkable, and local news wanted to know how she did it. When asked during graduation, Ashley pointed to a special teacher. Ashley said, "She constantly challenged me. Her difficult assignments challenged me academically. She stretched me and showed me just how far my abilities could go."

She continued, "My teacher challenged me in ways I've never been challenged before. I have discovered things about myself that I never knew before."

SELF-KNOWLEDGE AND KNOWLEDGE OF GOD

A fashion magazine was interviewing a group of British actors, and they discussed the challenge of speaking with an American accent in various Hollywood movies. The interviewer decided to flip the script and ask who they thought did the worst British accent in a movie. Several names were mentioned, but one name came up over and over again: Dick Van Dyke in Mary Poppins.

Evidently, word got around to Dick Van Dyke that his British accent in the movie was less than compelling. People asked him why his British accent was so awful. His answer was that no one told him.

To make matters worse, he was surrounded the entire time by a British cast, but no one bothered to mention it to him. Years later, Dick Van Dyke asked Julie Andrews, who played the title role as Mary Poppins, "'Why didn't you tell me?' She said it was because [he] was working so hard."[7]

It can be unsettling to realize that everyone in the room knows about your flaw, but that they keep it to themselves and never mention it to you. Like Dick Van Dyke, you might continue your work with the presumption that everything was all right.

We live in a society where people are reluctant to correct someone for fear of giving offense. More than ever in history, divergent groups exist in tribal communities or "echo chambers"—insulated, self-reinforcing worlds where people share the same biases, opinions, and interests. Social media often provides a forum for people to find their own echo chambers.

When everyone in the echo chamber is saying the same thing and repeating it over and over, any deviation from the established script will seem preposterous. In addition to perceiving the world from one narrow point of view, the proliferation of echo chambers, according to one social psychologist, "threaten our democratic conversation, splitting up the common ground of assumption and fact that is needed for diverse people to talk to each other."[8]

There are many instances in the Gospels where Jesus challenged people's assumptions. The way he did this may seem unusual, but it stirred their faith anyway.

In Luke 5:1-11, Jesus challenges Peter to go back to the lake and fish after Peter had spent the whole night fishing but catching very little. At first, Peter thought the idea was crazy. He had been fishing there for many years and probably thought, "He is a carpenter. Who is he to tell me how to fish?" By challenging Peter to do something that did not make complete sense, Jesus asked Peter to trust him. Peter accepted Jesus' challenge.

Peter replied, "'Master, we have worked hard all night long but have caught nothing. Yet if you say so, I will let down the nets'" (5:5). Then the most spectacular thing happened. Peter and his friends caught so many fish that the nets were about to break. Imagine the scene in your mind and the shocked look on Peter's face. He trusted God and accepted the challenge and learned something he never knew.

FOCUS AND DISCERNMENT

Once upon a time, a bunch of frogs in the rainforest fell into in a large hole. They all looked up from the bottom and groaned, "We'll never get out! We're in too deep! Not a chance anyone can make it out!" said the first frog. "Way too difficult! Anyone who tries is a fool!" added a second. "No one can make it! It's too hard," reiterated a third.

While the other frogs were talking, one frog jumped and began climbing. He slid down the side and the other frogs began to make fun of him. This did not deter him. He jumped again and slide down again and again, but he just kept climbing and climbing.

Finally, after a long struggle, he climbed out of the hole. Once he got out, the frog helped every other frog out of the hole.

All of the other frogs were speechless. They were absolutely amazed that he did what they all thought was impossible and they wanted to know how this one frog managed to do it.

As it turned out, the young frog who got out was deaf. He could not hear what everyone else was saying. He could not hear all the negativity, snarky remarks, and peer pressure. All he could hear was his inner voice saying that he needed to get out of the hole no matter the odds and help others to get out.[9]

If the chatter is all that we hear, we can be left discouraged. Study is an opportunity for us to listen more closely, and in doing so, fix our ears to the voice of the shepherd among the noise. We live in the most technologically advanced period in human history, but we also experience an unprecedented amount of chatter.

The spiritual practice of study helps us develop discernment. If chatter is all that we listen to, we will have difficulty recognizing clear directions. When we study, we focus our attention on the Lord and away from the chatter. As we study more, our ability to discern increases. It helps us to see things better, more clearly.

In Christian circles, *discernment* has become a popular word. The term comes from the Latin word *discerne*, which means "to separate, to distinguish, to sort out." Christian discernment is about sifting through the myriad of voices around us to focus on the voice of God. Study helps us focus on God's voice.

In John 10:27, Jesus says, "My sheep hear my voice . . . and they follow me." His sheep are able to discern one shepherd from another "because they know his voice" (v. 4). The sheep are locked in to their shepherd; they "will not follow a stranger" because "they do not know the voice of strangers" (v. 5).

Study helps us to discern the voice of the shepherd. Proverbs 4:23 states, "Be careful how you think; your life is shaped by your thoughts" (GNT). The spiritual practice of study helps shift our focus more to God than the noise that surrounds us.

Our life is shaped by our thoughts. We are susceptible to what we hear and, unfortunately, we hear a lot more chatter now due to social media. We become what we believe about ourselves. If we align what we think and believe according to the world then we will be shaped by those thoughts.

The frog who got out was the deaf frog—the one who didn't hear all the negativity and pressure about how he couldn't do it. Because he could not hear, he did not believe in all the negativity.

Imagine if your belief in God was so strong and so deep that you believed no matter what. I think this is what Jesus was talking about when he said if you have faith as small as a mustard seed, you can move mountains. If we want to succeed, we need to be careful about what kind of thoughts are living inside of us.

There are many different types of thoughts as well. There are kind thoughts, affirming thoughts, and thoughts that bring us warmth and a sense of pride. There are also thoughts that try to condemn us and bring us down, thoughts that make us ashamed or embarrassed, and thoughts that attempt to belittle us or suck the joy out of our lives.

Too often, people today listen to the world. Too often, people live with thoughts that tell them that they are no good and will never succeed. But that's not what God tells us. In Philippians 1:9, Paul writes, "This is my prayer that your love may overflow more and more with knowledge and full insight to help you to determine what is best."

STUDY AS QUEST FOR GOD

The spiritual practice of study makes our faith come alive. That is what this book is all about, understanding study as an instrument of fellowship with God. Study is an emotional expression of the soul—an expression of desired fellowship and closeness with God. Let study be a tender expression of the pursuit of a deeper appreciation and understanding of God.

Biblical writers, especially in Psalms, expressed their passions to God. Psalm 84:1-2 says,

> How lovely is your dwelling place,
>   O Lord of hosts!
> My soul longs, indeed it faints
>   for the courts of the Lord;
> my heart and my flesh sing for joy
>   to the living God.

By studying and gaining understanding, we approach the court of the Lord to experience God's presence. We get a taste of the goodness of the Lord and we long for more. As Psalm 84 goes on to say,

> For a day in your courts is better
>   than a thousand elsewhere.
> I would rather be a doorkeeper in the house of
>   my God
>   than live in the tents of wickedness. (v. 10)

The call to study is an active process that involves our mind, our emotions, and our spirit. In today's culture, we are more accustomed to passive learning. We sit back and receive entertainment and don't engage it directly. Instead of a passive experience, the spiritual practice of study provokes us to grapple with the insight, meanings, and nuances of what we discover.

AUTHORITY AND CONFIDENCE IN CHRIST

There is an old story about a farmer who found an eagle's egg. The farmer took it home with him and put the egg into a nest with eggs from his chickens. The eaglet eventually hatched along with the neighboring chicks. Surrounded by chicks, the eaglet did what the chickens did. The eaglet scratched in the dirt for seeds and insects to eat. He clucked and cackled. After all, that's what chickens were supposed to do, and he assumed he was a chicken.

Years passed, and the eagle grew very old. One day, he saw a magnificent bird far above him in the sky. With outstretched wings, the bird soared through the winds and rose higher and higher.

Amazed, the eagle marveled to his fellow chicken, "What a beautiful bird!" What is it? The chicken replied, "That my friend is the eagle . . . the grandest of all birds." The chicken saw that his friend greatly admired the eagle and said, "Don't give it another thought. You could never be like him."

And so, the eagle never gave it another thought. He died thinking and acting like a chicken.[10]

The spiritual practice of study will help us to realize that we are not chickens, but rather eagles who are meant to soar. The confidence we generate from our study will enable us to soar higher and higher in our faith. We will be able soar above our fears and anxieties, the way God intended.

In Isaiah 40:27, the prophet addresses a complaint to God, "My right is disregarded by my God." The immediate response in verse 28 is: "Have you not known?" Isaiah felt abandoned by God and was depressed and distressed as a result. However, from God's perspective, the prophet simply did not know.

"Have you not known? Have you not heard?" is the question posed to the downtrodden. God continues:

> The LORD is the everlasting God,
> the Creator of the ends of the earth.
> He does not faint or grow weary;
> his understanding is unsearchable.
> . . . .
> Even youths will faint and be weary,
> and the young will fall exhausted.
> (Isaiah 40:28-30)

On their own, even youths—with all their vigor and optimism—will eventually grow tired, weary, and distressed

> but those who wait for the LORD shall renew their strength,
> they shall mount up with wings like eagles,

> they shall run and not be weary,
>> they shall walk and not faint. (Isaiah 40:31).

The same question is presented to us, "Do you not know? Have you not heard?"

Because it is posed in the form of a question, it makes us think about ourselves and contemplate what we do not know. This is the kind of critical thinking that study sparks in the reader. Study gets us to imagine feeling the exuberance of "mounting up with wings like eagles." The Bible uses visual language to illustrate the confidence that God wants to instill within us.

"Do you not know?"

The question awakens us to a new reality beyond what we are feeling at the moment. The knowledge of God stimulates us to soul-searching reflection of higher reality that will deliver us to new heights.

Many people today are experiencing high levels of anxiety. Here are just a few headlines from recent years:

- "Depression Diagnosis Up 47% Among Millennials"
- "Millennials: The Most Anxious Generation, New Research Shows"
- "Millennials at Higher Risk for Mental High Issues"
- "Most U.S. Teens See Anxiety and Depression as a Major Problem Among Their Peers."[11]

An article titled "Mental Health Among Millennials at All Time High" focused on an interesting diagnosis for the situation. While it mentioned the ill-effects of social media and obsession with technology as possible causes for mental health issues, the report noted psychologists who pointed out that "uncertainty of the future . . . impacts students the most."[12] According to a survey by British researchers, 86 percent of millennials say they are in a quarter-life crisis. Similarly, a 2018 report stated that millennials had seen a 47 percent increase in depression diagnoses.[13] Many call the millennials the "burnout generation" as they face a host of mental and spiritual challenges.

"Do you not know?" may be a question that God is asking.

God reminds us over and over that this is not the end of the story. Those who wait upon the Lord will rise up. Studying and understanding God's character increases our confidence.

Here are several benefits of studying as a spiritual practice:

- We feel refreshed
- We can face the day's challenges more confidently
- We develop a greater sense of peace, joy, contentment, gratitude, calm
- We discover a deeper understanding of ourselves and our faith
- We more clearly see God's handiwork in the world and in our lives
- We gain clarity when making life decisions

The knowledge of God stimulates new possibilities. When we study, it's like our spiritual tanks fill with fuel. The worries of this world are numerous, but the spiritual practice of study acts as a constant reminder of the goodness of the Lord.

STUDY

Questions for Personal Reflection and Group Discussion

1. What words fill your life? What are some of the positive words that fill up your life? What are some of the negative ones? Who is reinforcing these words? What words do you think God has to say about you?

2. What values do you think lie at the heart of God? How do God's interactions with people help us understand what God finds important? How does study help us to learn more about these values and put them into practice in our lives?

3. What examples from our society can you think of that exhibit our desire to know? Do you feel this desire to know is universal? How does your desire to know express itself?

4. How does study help us to understand ourselves more? How does it help us to become more self-aware? How do understanding and self-awareness play out in our faith?

CHAPTER 4

Study as Life-long Pursuit

OPENING PRAYER

Ask, and it will be given you; search, and you will find; knock, and the door will be opened for you. For everyone who asks receives, and everyone who searches finds, and for everyone who knocks, the door will be opened. Is there anyone among you who, if your child asks for bread, will give a stone? Or if the child asks for a fish, will give a snake? If you then, who are evil, know how to give good gifts to your children, how much more will your Father in heaven give good things to those who ask him! (Matthew 7:7-11)

SULLY

The name "Sully" Sullenberger has found a place in our collective memory. On January 15, 2009, Sullenberger was the captain of US Airways Flight 1549. Just after the flight left LaGuardia airport in New York City, the plane was struck by a flock of Canadian geese and the plane's engines were left without any power. The plane needed to make an emergency landing; but where do you do that in New York City? Captain Sullenberger, or "Sully" as he is commonly known, quickly determined that neither returning to LaGuardia nor trying to reach Teterboro airport in New Jersey were feasible options. He had flown for more than 40 years and accumulated 20,000 hours of flight experience, but this problem was unique. In fact, the circumstances were so unique that they were not even included on flight simulators, which are intended to expose pilots to every kind of emergency and adverse condition.

There was only one option: the Hudson River. But how do you land a plane on a river when you have never trained for it? The scenario presented a stark life-or-death outcome. The slightest error would have been a disaster. For example, if the plane did not land evenly, with both engines in the water at the same time, one wingtip would have hit the water first and plane would have done a disastrous cartwheel.

Yet on that day, Sully was perfect, and all 155 people aboard the plane survived. The media dubbed the landing "The Miracle on the Hudson," and the indelible image of passengers standing patiently on the plane's wings, waiting for the ferries to rescue them, is etched in our minds. The National Transportation Safety Board called the response of the piloting crew "the most successful ditching in aviation history."[1]

All pilots, even beginners, can fly a plane in mild, sunny weather; but what happens when unpredictable, wild, and bizarre situations take place? What about when life throws us a wild curveball, how do we handle it? What do we fall back on?

The answer is knowledge. Sully had never encountered this situation and had never prepared for it, but he managed to make the best decision and execute an unorthodox maneuver perfectly.

One often overlooked part of this story is that Sully is also a certified glider pilot. Gliders are engineless planes. Gilder pilots land or "glide" their planes without any motor power. When Flight 1549 lost both of its engines shortly after leaving LaGuardia, it began to glide over New York City. Because glider planes have no engines, they are light, weighing 200-450 pounds. In this scenario, Sully was flying an Airbus A320, which is a 70-ton airplane, fully loaded with passengers, luggage, and fuel. In a moment like that, there is little time to think, and you have to grasp for every possible thing that you know and hold it tight.

By all accounts, Sully was a senior pilot with a reputable record but, when the situation called for him to step up, he rose to extraordinary. His knowledge of gliding a plane as well as the countless hours of experience allowed Sully to create a new approach that has never been done before; in the process, he saved the lives of his passengers and crew. Sully could never have imagined such a scenario, but his knowledge was the precious resource that allowed him to think and move quickly into action.

The spiritual practice of study encourages us to soak up all the knowledge that God has made available. In the process, it brings us rich insights into the meaning of life and what it means to be a child of God. Proverbs 20:15 declares, "There is gold, and abundance of costly stones; / but the lips informed by knowledge are a precious jewel." In other words, wealth is great, but knowledge is worth much more. This isn't the only time Proverbs makes this point either. In Proverbs 8:10, the writer directs readers to "Take my instruction instead of silver, / and knowledge rather than choice gold." Scripture encourages us to value study as an integral part of life for "knowledge will be pleasant to your soul (Proverbs 2:10)."

The Lord has made wisdom and knowledge available to all who seek them, but we must make the effort to acquire them. These efforts start with pursuing God. "The fear of the Lord is the beginning of wisdom, / and the knowledge of the Holy One is insight," announces Proverbs 9:10.

MAINTAIN A HABIT OF STUDY

For a time, I pastored a small church in Pennsylvania Dutch country. One of the members there was a woman in her eighties whom everyone called Grandma. She was a petite woman, but her diminutive appearance belied the dynamo that she was.

Every morning, Grandma got up before anyone else and was running at full speed all day long. She made bread, cakes, and German pies from scratch, knew every traditional home remedy there was to know, and worked the dairy farm right alongside the rest of her family.

She also made a point of staying fit both physically and spiritually. She believed that a person needed to work his or her muscles every day in order to maintain a high level of fitness. In order to get in a spiritual workout, she kept to a strict regimen of prayer and Bible reading every day. Her faith was based on simple and time-worn common sense: when we exercise our spiritual muscles, it makes us stronger and healthier. She was an inspiration to the church and reminded all of us of the importance of maintaining healthy habits.

In order to maximize the benefits of study as a spiritual practice, we need to look at it as a long-term investment. If we don't commit ourselves to study on a regular basis, it can easily fall by the wayside. While there will always be moments of frustration, we must remember that there is also much to be gained.

Getting started tends to be the hardest part for many people. Getting the mind in gear requires focus and effort. However, when we establish a habit of practice, it becomes nearly automatic. After some time and with some discipline, study becomes a part of our routine.

AT YOUR OWN PACE AND PLACE
> When you have a habit of practicing at the same time and in the same place every day, you hardly have to think about getting started. You just do.[2]

Look over your weekly schedule. Ask yourself when you can devote regular time to study. If our schedules seem full, we may need to consider how we can make room, such as cutting back on social media or TV.

Would a short study before we start the day help us center our thoughts on God? Or is there time in the middle of the day when we can find moments without distraction? Perhaps the evening is the best option as the day is winding down. The time is not important, but the rhythm and habit of regular study is, and each of us needs to find what works best.

Finding the right space is also essential. You might be the type of person who flourishes when studying in a bustling coffee shop or some other public space. When I was a student in New York City, I studied well while riding in a crowded subway for some reason. If a crowded space is more of a distraction, solitude and silence in a local library might be helpful. Whatever your learning style, take the time to ensure that your location is where you can work without distractions.

The internet can also be a major obstacle for many of us. Checking our social media feeds and emails, watching videos, and just generally bouncing from site to site has become second nature for many of us.

Because it's so omnipresent, it can be a serious barrier to study. When you embrace the study of spiritual practice, commit to putting away your devices or turning off your wi-fi to help you focus.

When we hit our groove, study can feel like a plane soaring in the sky, free and easy. However, before a plane can fly, it needs to take off. Some of us never get to experience the joy of flight because we are stuck on the runway. We power on the engine and move forward to liftoff, but we get distracted and lose our momentum. When we decide to check email or social media for a quick update, we lose power. When this happens, we have to turn the plane around and start over at the beginning.

Give yourself the best chance to achieve liftoff. Find a good time, a comfortable space, and do your best to avoid distractions. If you have not studied for years, start slowly. If you are having difficulty getting started, consider committing 15 minutes to study at first and then slowly increase your time.

Don't get discouraged if you don't make it off the runway in the beginning. The engine may need more time to power up to the necessary speed. Just be aware of what's keeping you from the task of studying. There may be days when you achieve liftoff and others when the engine stalls. The important thing is to keep your commitment to study. If we expect too much in the beginning, we may burn out before we are ready.

STUDY AS A LIFE-LONG PURSUIT

The more we study and the more we examine, the more knowledge we collect and the more we grow to understand God's will. There is no telling how far we can go. At the same time, if we choose to ignore learning, there are implications for that as well.

One story from the American Civil War reminds us of both the importance of knowledge and the consequences of ignoring it. Over the five years of fighting, a mind-boggling 620,000 men lost their lives. To put it into perspective, one out of every 50 people living in the United States at the time died in the fighting. The casualties from the Battle of Gettysburg alone totaled over 51,000, a figure higher than the Revolutionary War, the War of 1812, and the Mexican-American War combined.[3]

In hindsight, many of us would be shocked to learn that most of these deaths could have been easily prevented. Incredibly, more soldiers died from disease than from battle wounds. For every soldier who died in battle, two died of disease. About half of the deaths were caused by typhoid fever, diarrhea, and dysentery. Diarrhea and dysentery alone killed more men than actual battles.

How was this possible? How did disease spread so fast? We get some clarity on this situation from an inspector who traveled around surveying army camps. He observed that the camps were "littered with refuse, food, and other rubbish, sometimes in an offensive state of decomposition; slops deposited in pits within the camp limits or thrown out of broadcast; heaps of manure and offal close to the camp."[4]

In other words, tens of thousands of men in army camps lived among heaps of garbage along with human and animal waste. The filthy conditions unleashed an infestation of rodents and mosquitoes carrying deadly germs and bacteria.

The simple explanation for this tragic situation was that the people of the time simply didn't know what they were doing. They did not know that building camps in damp areas exposed soldiers to malaria. They did not know that crowding soldiers together in cramped living conditions fostered the spread of diseases. They did not know that unnecessary exposure to other sick people could turn a simple cold into a case of pneumonia.

Surgeons, due to a shortage of water in the camps, performed surgeries without washing their hands or their medical instruments, thereby passing on germs from one patient to the next and spreading deadly infections to healthy soldiers suffering from minor ailments. They did not know the simple practices of hygiene and sterilization that would have saved hundreds of thousands of lives. One researcher on the Civil War wrote, "Nothing was known about how and why wounds became infected. . . . The number of men who simply got sick and died, or who got a minor scratch or cut and then could do nothing to check the infection was appalling."[5]

Those in charge had no malicious intent, but their lack of knowledge had far-reaching consequences in ways they could not have imagined. Had they possessed this knowledge, they would have been able to put in place safeguards to ensure the health and safety of the men they were responsible for.

This story illustrates the dangers of what we don't know and forces us to ask what simple things we might be overlooking in our own lives. What if the toils and hardships of life could be averted if we knew how to address them? What if we have only scratched the surface of what God wants us to know? What if we are missing out on a treasure trove of knowledge that would help us grow closer to God and understand what God desires for the world?

HOSEA

Hosea, a prophet in the Old Testament, had a major gripe with the Israelites because they rejected knowledge of God. Hosea declared,

> Hear the word of the LORD, O people of Israel;
> for the Lord has an indictment against the
> inhabitants of the land.
> There is no faithfulness or loyalty,
> and no knowledge of God in the land.
> (Hosea 4:1)

This indictment isn't exclusive to Hosea; it is found throughout Scripture. Psalm 82:5 tells us,

> They have neither knowledge nor understanding,
> they walk around in darkness;
> all the foundations of the earth are shaken.

Similarly, Proverbs 1:22 chimes in saying,

> How long, O simple ones, will you love being
> simple?
> How long will scoffers delight in their scoffing
> and fools hate knowledge?

In the verses that follow Hosea 4:1, the prophet declares that those who have "no knowledge of God" (v. 1) have "forgotten the law" (v. 6). Without the knowledge of God to guide and lead them, the people are essentially left to their own devices. God made this knowledge easily accessible to the people, but they refused to accept it. Observing the suffering and self-destruction that had come to God's people as a result of their rejection of God's knowledge, a heart-broken Hosea cries out "My people are destroyed for lack of knowledge" (v. 6).

This may leave us wondering how people can be destroyed for a lack of knowledge. Is knowledge truly this important for our well-being?

To answer the question simply: knowledge could save your life.

In March 2019, reports from Spokane, Washington surfaced about two sisters, ages five and eight, who survived being lost in the wilderness for nearly two days. The girls were playing on their family's 80-acre property when they wandered off and got lost. For an adult, two days in the wilderness might be uncomfortable, but for two young children it could be deadly. How did these children make it on their own?

The answer: two years of survival training. Do you know the most important factors for survival? If you immediately thought food, then you are sorely mistaken. Food is not the highest priority, because human beings can go without food for at least three weeks. However, humans can't go even three days without water. Furthermore, you can last only about three hours without shelter in harsh, adverse weather conditions.

Fortunately, the girls knew the three basic, but crucial elements for survival: fire, water, and shelter. This knowledge about how to survive was ingrained in the children at a young age. They know how to get water, how to start a fire to keep warm, and how to build a shelter.

Now, imagine if these girls or anyone else was lost in the wilderness without this knowledge. Left to their own devices, they may assume that finding food is the priority. They are used to eating three meals a day plus snacks, and they are feeling hungry. As they become desperate, they expend most of their energy finding food, all the while ignoring more pressing matters. They may survive, but their chances have dropped considerably.

In another story of survival, years ago a student got caught in a terrible snowstorm in Minnesota. The blizzard made it hazardous for cars to travel, and many motorists were stuck on the road. The student knew the blizzard was going to last a while, so she ripped up her car-seat, taking the stuffing from the seats and used it to insulate herself further underneath her coat. She walked miles before she finally reached help. Eventually the blizzard passed, many who were in the same situation as the student froze to death in their vehicles.

A highway official commenting on the situation remarked, "If you are stuck in the harsh winter, your survival depends on *what you know*."

In the beginning of his second letter, the apostle Peter prays that "grace and peace be yours in abundance in the knowledge of God and of Jesus our Lord" (2 Peter 1:2). Peter declared that God's "divine power has given us everything needed for life and godliness, through the knowledge of him (v. 3)." Peter's desire was for Christians to "become participants of the divine nature" (v. 4), and gaining knowledge of God was an important step in this participation.

In many aspects of life, gaining knowledge can make us arrogant or lead us to feel superior to others. The knowledge of God, however, has the opposite effect. The knowledge of God will humble us. In his commentary on 2 Peter 1:6, John Wesley wrote, "The more knowledge [of God] you have, the more renounce your own will; indulge yourself the less."[6] In other words, the more Christians understand God and the path toward godliness, the more restraint Christians exercise.

STUDY TO REST IN GOD

A 2018 newspaper headline read, "The U.S. Is the Most Overworked Developed Nation in the World." Yes, *the* world. Americans work longer hours than anyone else. According to the International Labour Organization (ILO), "Americans work 137 more hours per year than Japanese workers, 260 more hours per year than British workers, and 499 more hours per year than French workers."[7]

There may be some of us who absolutely love our jobs and can't wait to go to work, but for most of us more work means more stress and less time we can spend to cultivate our inner life. Without time to unwind, to spend with loved ones, and to connect with and enjoy our friends, it can be difficult to live an enriching life.

Needless to say, most of us experience an unhealthy amount of stress. Stress is the number one cause of health problems, both mentally and physically. The American Heart Association reports that stress may even increase the risk of heart disease, the leading killer of Americans.[8]

In this overwhelming whirlwind, the spiritual practice of study can provide us with a way to combat stress and find peace in the Lord. Take Psalm 23:1-4 for instance:

> The Lord is my shepherd, I shall not want.
>   He makes me lie down in green pastures;
> he leads me beside still waters;
>   he restores my soul.

He leads me in right paths
    for his name's sake.

Even though I walk through the darkest valley,
    I fear no evil;
for you are with me;
    your rod and your staff—
    they comfort me.

Note the concept of the shepherd found here. Note all of the different roles of the shepherd. Then go deeper. Seriously, take out your phones and search "shepherds in the ancient world." Take note of all the various things that shepherds did.

Your search likely revealed to you that shepherds fed, protected, loved, led, cared for, defended, and at times even lived with their sheep.

David, the author of Psalm 23, was a shepherd for most of his early life. Perhaps more than any other biblical author, he knew what it took to be a shepherd. Consider David's usage of "shepherd" to describe God. Examine and note what David could have been thinking and feeling.

Jesus extends this shepherd metaphor in John 10:11-15 and used it to describe himself:

I am the good shepherd. The good shepherd lays down his life for the sheep. The hired hand, who is not the shepherd and does not own the sheep, sees the wolf coming and leaves the sheep and runs away—and the wolf snatches them and scatters them. The hired hand runs away because a hired hand does not care for the sheep. I am the good shepherd. I know my own and my own know me, just as the Father knows me and I know the Father. And I lay down my life for the sheep.

With our prior understanding of what it means to be a shepherd, let alone a good shepherd, the meaning of this verse deepens, and we learn even more about how God cares for us and loves us.

In studying passages and concepts like this, we see how study can be an opportunity to meet God. Through our studies, we are invited to hear, explore, and understand who God is. In John 4:10, Jesus said he is the "living water"; study allows us to draw on that spring as much as we would like.

The spiritual practice of study goes beyond learning facts, dates, and events to the way we connect with God on a personal level. In turn, God responds to our study and we enter into an authentic conversation with God.

By practicing study as a spiritual discipline, we aim to:

- Learn more about ourselves
- Grow in faith
- Become more intimate with God
- Discover more of God
- Become teachable to God's guidance and discipline
- Experience the riches of God's grace

OVERCOME EXPECTATION OF INSTANT RESULTS

Many of us will face the temptation to give up and quit our studies before giving them a chance to take hold. "It takes too long," someone might say, or maybe "I don't have the time for it." There is some truth in these statements; study does take time, but the time is worth it.

When we think about study, we should think of it as a marathon—not a sprint. The start of a marathon

and a sprint look very different. In a marathon, everyone is relaxed and standing around at the starting
line. When the race starts, everyone begins jogging in
a relaxed manner. Sprinters, on the other hand, start
crouched in a position that will allow for maximum
propulsion. Their faces look serious, and their muscles
are tense. At the sound of the gun, they rocket out of
their stance.

If we take view study as a sprint, we will quickly
get burned out. The reason marathon runners are
so relaxed at the beginning of a race is because they
know it's a very long race and sprinting out of the gate
will actually do more damage than good.

Most of us, however, are trained to have a sprint
mentality. We live in a culture that encourages us to
expect instant results and gratification. We are promised everything when we want it. The examples are
endless; fast-food, one-day delivery, and 15-minute
oil changes abound. In the aisles of your local super-
market you can find instant iced tea, instant soup mix,
and instant pancake mix. If we don't know something,
we Google it to find an answer. The future of artificial
intelligence promises that it will figure out what we
want before we even know we want it. In this society
of instant gratification, it's no wonder that we have
lost patience for long, drawn-out stories and the effort
it takes to reap their rewards.

Our sprint mentality has severe consequences for
our Christian faith. Following our culture, Christians
also expect revelation to come after short bursts of
intense experiences; many of us have lost the patience
to wait for the Lord's response to manifest in our lives.
Yet we would do well to remember the words of Isaiah
40:31:

Those who wait for the Lord shall renew their
strength,
they shall mount up with wings like eagles,
they shall run and not be weary,
they shall walk and not faint.

The spiritual practice of study requires the mentality of a marathoner. In other words, it requires discipline.

In the 1960s, a team of psychologists conducted a study of the importance of self-discipline and self-restraint. The experiment, famously known as the "marshmallow experiment" was done on a group of four-year-old children. Each of the children was placed in a room and was given a marshmallow. The psychologist would then tell the child that they would be given a second marshmallow if they could wait 20 minutes to eat the first one. At this point, the psychologist would leave the room.

Some of the children could not resist the sweet sugary goodness and gobbled up the marshmallow soon after the researcher left the room. Other children did resist for the required 20 minutes, but it wasn't easy. The hidden camera in the room showed the children squirming in their seats fighting the urge. To avoid thinking about the marshmallow some of them started singing or playing games—anything to stop them from staring at the marshmallow.

After 14 years, the psychologists tracked down the children that took the test to determine if there were any differences between those who resisted and those who couldn't resist. The researchers were surprised at the results because the differences were so stark. Those who were able to resist were more confident and motivated and better able to cope with the frustrations of life. In addition, the researchers suggested that their high academic achievement was gained through the ability to delay gratification and develop self-control. Both contributed significantly to their chances to read their full potential.[9]

We can expect instant gratification from our culture, but if we expect instant results from God, we will be disappointed. God will work on God's own timeline. There are hundreds of things that we can receive in an instant, but the fruit of study is not one of them. The rewards of study do not come today. They do not come tomorrow; they may not even come next week. But they will come in time, when God wants them to.

Study as a spiritual practice is a marathon. Like a marathon, we need patience, a relaxed disposition, and a long-term outlook.

STUDY GETS BETTER WITH PRACTICE

The renowned classical pianist Arthur Rubinstein said that he would never go a day without practicing on his piano. If he did, he said that the quality of his playing would at once begin to deteriorate. He said that after missing one day he would notice, after two days his friends would notice, and after just three days the public would notice as well.[10]

Studying is difficult, especially in the beginning when we are trying to turn it into a habit and find a place for it in our weekly schedule. Over time though, the initial hurdles and growing pains will slowly ebb, and we will notice that the work can be completed with greater ease.

To help us to see studying as a long-term venture, consider this story from a pastor's son about a 150-year old farmhouse in Vermont. The old house did not have electricity, gas, or plumbing, but the son remembered his family being happy. Eventually the family moved away, but the son—now an adult with a family of his own—remembered the old well near the front door of the house.

The well was one of those old-fashioned hand-crank wells; you had to press down hard to pump the water up. He fondly remembered the well for a couple of reasons. First, the water from the well was delicious. It was always cold, pure, and a bit sweet. Second, the water from the well never ran dry—even in summer droughts when other families in the area would have to go to the lake for their drinking water.

When the family's situation improved, they decided to modernize the house. Electricity replaced the old kerosene lamps, an electric stove took over from the ancient kerosene burner, and modern plumbing and running water were installed.

With plumbing installed in the house, that old well was no longer needed, and it was covered up. Soon, the kids grew up and moved out. Many years later, after he had grown up and had kids of his own, the son returned to the old farmhouse to show his kids the rustic home where he grew up. He wanted his kids to taste that cold and sweet well water. He uncovered the well and started pumping and pumping, but nothing came out. It was bone dry. All it pumped was dust and air.

Completely baffled by the well that had never gone dry before, he started to ask everyone in his neighborhood how this happened. He discovered that the well was fed by hundreds of tiny underground channels, called rivulets, along which seeps a constant supply of water. As water is drawn, more water moves along the tiny channels, keeping the tiny channels clear and open.

However, if the well is not used and the water is not regularly drawn, the tiny channels slowly close up and eventually the well itself dries up. The underground water was still there, but the channels to receive it were closed.

When we begin our journey of study, it may appear that we are only receiving a few droplets of knowledge. But, with patience and perseverance, the amount that we receive will slowly increase as the tiny channels open wider. Once a steady stream of cold, refreshing water flows, it is important to keep in mind that continuous practice is necessary to keep the flow going.

LET IT SHAPE YOUR CHARACTER

In Victor Hugo's classic novel, *Les Misérables*, the main character Jean Valjean is despondent when he is first introduced. Imprisoned for stealing bread, Valjean served many years of hard labor and he carries the aura of a hardened criminal. A recently released convict, Valjean is rejected by everyone in town. He says to himself, "I am not even a dog."[11]

As he tries to find a bed for the night, no one shows him any kindness. Finally, a woman in the village directs Valjean to the bishop's home. Perhaps he will show compassion. The bishop answers the door, and immediately Valjean confesses his prison time and reveals his criminal past saying, "There is my passport, yellow as you see. That is enough to have me kicked out wherever I go." The bishop replies, "Monsieur, sit down and warm yourself: we are going to take supper presently, and your bed will be made ready while you sup."[12]

But Valjean is not yet prepared to live a life on the straight and narrow. In the middle of the night, Valjean steals the bishop's silver and runs away, only to be caught by the local police who bring him back to the bishop's home. Valjean expects the bishop to confirm that he is a low-life thief, but the bishop shocks Valjean with his response, "I am glad to see you. But! I gave you the candlesticks also, which are silver like the rest, and would bring two hundred francs."[13]

Valjean is shaken to his core and speechless at this act of generosity. The bishop brings over the silver candlesticks and whispers to Valjean, "Forget not, never forget you have promised me to use this silver to become an honest man."[14] The bishop's unmerited mercy forever changes Valjean. Turning his life around completely, Valjean goes on to own a factory and become a wealthy man. More importantly, he spends much of his fortune helping the city and the poor.

The words of the bishop stayed with Valjean, guided his actions and shaped his future. Those words transformed Valjean into a new person. What a difference words can make. In a similar way, the practice of study reinforces God's words in our hearts. We let them take roots and allow them to bear fruit. Study as a spiritual practice cultivates the soil of our hearts, making them fertile so that seeds from God will harvest and "produce a hundredfold (Luke 8:8)."

Valjean had an awful view of himself. He was a convict. He saw himself as a cold, hardened criminal with little redeeming value. Society saw him as a monster. But not the bishop. The bishop redeemed Valjean and gave him new life. Paul echoes this message in 2 Corinthians 5:17, "So if anyone is in Christ, there is a new creation: everything old has passed away; see, everything has become new!"

God changes the way we think about ourselves. Study as spiritual practice provides both a means of conversing with God and of coming to terms with God's wisdom. In God's many encounters with humanity in the Bible, God sees beyond the labels that people have placed upon themselves and accepted from others and elevates them above their reality.

Moses is considered to be one of the greatest leaders in history, yet, in the beginning of the story, when God appointed Moses to lead his people out of slavery, Moses was terrified and could not understand what God saw in him. Moses cowered, "O my Lord, I have never been eloquent, neither in the past nor even now that you have spoken to your servant; but I am slow of speech and slow of tongue . . . O my Lord, please send someone else" (Exodus 4:10-13).

God remained firm and insisted that Moses rise above his fears and reservations to do what he was called to do. God calls us to do the same. Instead of seeing ourselves the way God sees us, we have a habit of focusing on our problems, our deficiencies, our shortcomings, and our insecurities. Moses was just like us. We prefer to stay in the comfort of the shadows rather than boldly walking into the light.

What we learn through study prods us to consider the way God sees us, and the not the way the world sees us. In 1 Samuel 16, God instructed Samuel to go to Bethlehem where God would show him the next king of Israel. At this point, Samuel knew that one of Jesse's sons was the anointed one, but he didn't know which son; and Jesse had eight sons. When the sons arrived to meet Samuel, one caught Samuel's eye. Samuel looked at Eliab and thought, "Surely the LORD's anointed is now before the LORD" (1 Samuel 16:6).

God read Samuel's mind. God saw that Samuel was very much impressed with Eliab's physique, handsomeness, and aura of leadership. God corrected Samuel's misguided priorities and told him, "Do not look on his appearance or on the height of his stature, because I have rejected him; for the Lord does not see as mortals see; they look on the outward appearance, but the Lord looks on the heart" (v. 7).

Our culture has a powerful influence on us, and our self-image is often marred by an increased attention to our physical appearance, social charms, and intellectual skills. Studying the way God sees us peels away the layers of misdirection provided by our cultural education. Study affords us the opportunity to get a real sense of how God views us.

Study also keeps us focused on what God thinks of us. In doing so, we are not defined by the number of "likes" on social media or the opinions of the world. Proverbs 3 begins, "My child, do not forget my teaching, / but let your heart keep my commandments." To ensure that you remember those words, the reader is instructed to "Bind them around your neck, / write them on the tablet of your heart" (v. 3).

Study aids us in our effort to hold God's thoughts and words in our hearts. The same metaphor is used again in Proverbs 7 when the writer says,

> My child, keep my words
>   and store up my commandments with you;
> keep my commandments and live,
>   keep my teachings as the apple of your eye;
> bind them on your fingers,
> write them on the tablet of your heart.
>
> (Proverbs 7:1-3)

TIGER AND RABBIT

The Korean peninsula is a largely mountainous region, and a long time ago many wild tigers inhabited the mountains and forests found there. There are also a number of Korean folktales about tigers. One story in particular describes what happened when a village got fed up with tigers attacking travelers in the nearby mountainside. In an effort to stop the tigers, the villagers decided to dig several pits around the outskirts of the village and then covered the pits with leaves.

One day, while a traveler was passing by, he heard a loud rustling noise in the leaves behind him. He went to investigate and discovered that a large tiger had fallen into one of the pits. Seeing the traveler, the tiger begged him for help, "Please, sir, help me out of this trap, and I will never forget your kindness." The traveler felt pity for the tiger, so he dragged over a felled tree and lowered it into the pit, which allowed the tiger to climb out.

The tiger was greatly pleased. He said to the traveler, "I am very grateful for your help, but because humans made the trap to catch me, for that I will have to kill you." The traveler immediately turned white in fear, but he gathered his wits quickly and replied, "Wait a minute, Mr. Tiger. You are right that humans made this trap, but at the same time I rescued you. It is only fair that we should ask a few impartial parties to judge the situation." The tiger thought about it and agreed.

Nearby, they saw an ox. After the listening to the scenario, the ox concluded, "Well, it is the fault of the humans. We, oxen, too, have a grudge against humans. They drive us hard every day to work in the fields and when we get too old, they butcher us and eat us! That is very unfair!"

Next, they went to a pine tree. After listening to the traveler and the tiger, the pine tree said, "Humans are in the wrong. They cut us down for lumber and for firewood! What have we done to them to deserve that! That is very unfair!"

After listening to the opinions of the ox and the pine tree, the tiger was delighted and prepared to pounce on the traveler. Then, at that exact moment, the traveler spotted a rabbit hopping past. The traveler pointed to the rabbit and said, "There's Mr. Rabbit. Let's ask him." Catching the rabbit's attention, the traveler said, "Mr. Rabbit, please give us your opinion on our case." He proceeded to explain the situation.

The rabbit replied, "In order to make the best judgment, I must carefully examine the scene of the incident where this all took place." The traveler, the tiger, and the rabbit all went to the deep pit where the tiger was trapped. Looking down at the pit, the rabbit said, "I see . . . Mr. Tiger, where were you exactly when the traveler found you?" Eager to show where he was, the tiger jumped into the pit.

"I see. Mr. Tiger, I notice this tree in the pit. Was this tree also there when you fell?" questioned the rabbit. "No, it was not," the tiger replied. Then, the rabbit said, "Let's get to the original condition." So the traveler and rabbit pulled the tree out of the pit.

With the tree out and the tiger in the pit, the rabbit said, "Mr. Traveler, now be on your way." And with that the rabbit simply hopped away.

When we find ourselves in a dire situation like the one the traveler was in, we must remember to never stop asking, thinking, and examining the world around us. We must continue to ask, seek, and knock in order to find the right answer. The spiritual practice of study helps us to nurture creative responses to the demands of life and provides us a forum to investigate different issues and problems. Johann Wolfgang von Goethe once said, "All truly wise thoughts have been thought already thousands of times but to make them truly ours, we must think them over again honestly, till they take root in our personal experience."[15]

In the ebb and flow of life, we face countless distractions and decisions. We are juggle many tasks and wear many hats. As a result, there are a number of things that can throw us off. How we adjust to life's unceasing challenges will determine how we respond to them.

I once read that the space shuttle is off-course 99 percent of the time, which is to say that it is off-course all of the time. When we think about that fact, it's not surprising; a space shuttle is, by design, drifting in space. The computers onboard the shuttle have to continuously trigger rockets to fire tiny bursts in order to make small adjustments that keep the spacecraft headed in the right direction.

Sometimes we may feel a little like the space shuttle, drifting along off course. When we study, we are triggering little adjustments to keep us lined up with our destination. If we drift by even one degree, we are off course. While the one degree won't make a huge difference in the beginning, the gap will slowly grow wider and wider. Before you know it, we are lost in space and very far from our destination.

Study can act as a kind of homing device. A homing device is a mechanism that guides the shuttle or any aircraft toward its objective. Study alerts us when we are off course and points to the direction of our destination. At a time when we maintain hectic schedules and lead chaotic lives, study as a spiritual practice brings us back to what is truly important and valuable.

STUDY

STUDY IN A GROUP

Obviously, you can study alone, but it's better to work as part of a group. The set-up allows group members to be both learners and teachers as they share, explain, and provide feedback about what they are learning. Successful study groups build community, accountability, and creativity. It can also allow for greater comprehension and enhanced fellowship.

There are a few keys to keep in mind when putting together a group:

- **Regular meetings.** If possible, try to meet on the same day and time each week. A regular meeting will help ensure that everyone has the time blocked off in their schedules. It's also important to set a longer timeframe for how long you will meet. Depending on the group's preference, a three- or four-month timeframe might work. Similarly, a limited seasonal study, such as during Advent or Lent may be an option.
- **Group size.** A study group of four to five people is ideal, but members can form a group that best suits their needs. For example, two friends can study together or two or three couples could form a couples' study. Any more than six and you may want to form two groups.
- **Group commitment.** The group can made up of friends, acquaintances, or strangers, but everyone in the group should be committed to the group's objectives and weekly schedule. You will be surprised to discover how others studying the same topic will draw out different insights or highlight something you missed.
- **Group decisions.** As a group, determine the topic, question, or narrative that the group

124

would like to explore together. There is no set time for how long you need to stay on each topic, so follow the flow of the discussions. For example, your group may discover an exciting topic and wish to stay on it for weeks.

- **Meeting place.** While you can always meet in someone's home, it may be helpful to consider other options as well. If your group needs a space free of distractions, consider meeting in a classroom at your church, or in a room at a local community center or library. If the group does not mind public settings, meeting at a coffee shop or diner might also work.
- **Group length.** Study groups should meet for about an hour. Making sure that your meetings end on time will ensure that everyone can keep their schedules.

Studying in a group stimulates your own learning. When you share your reflections, you are not only discussing your understanding of the material; you may also be educating others, especially if the material contains difficult concepts or passages. The process of discussing insights together forces us to consider fresh perspectives.

Educators have long known that studying with a group is one of the most effective ways to learn and process difficult material and concepts. From the beginning of formal education in the United States, when one-room schoolhouses were commonplace, group study was the fundamental way that students learned. Older students would teach young students, and study groups of similar level would work together to learn common material.

STUDY

STUDY TO *SHEW* THYSELF

As we conclude this book, I am reminded of Paul's instruction to Timothy in 2 Timothy 2:15, "Study to shew thyself approved unto God, a workman that needeth not to be ashamed, rightly dividing the word of truth" (KJV).

More modern translations obviously use different phrases. The NRSV and NIV both say, "Do your best to present yourself to God" and the NASB reads, "Be diligent to present yourself approved to God." The Message renders it as, "Concentrate on doing your best for God." But I am partial to the translation in the King James Version because it instructs us to *study*.

It's as if we are being asked to study ourselves along with our study of Scripture. We are holding a mirror up to ourselves and honestly asking, "Where am I in the sight of the Lord? Where do I stand? How am I doing?"

Studying oneself reminds me of John Wesley's Holy Club where members were required to ask themselves 22 Questions every day in their private devotions. The questions ranged from "Am I a hypocrite?" to "Can I be trusted?" Others included such incisive questions as "Did the Bible live in me today?" and "Is Christ real to me?"

As we consider how to embrace study as a spiritual practice, remember that study is not a walk in the park, nor is it meant to be. Instead, study, if done right, reaches for heavenly heights and grapples with eternal questions. In attempting to make sense of our own existence and purpose, study will produce something entirely satisfying. The rewards for study are substantial, but we have to take that first step.

STUDY AS LIFE-LONG PURSUIT

Questions for Personal Reflection and Group Discussion

1. What habits have you been able to incorporate over the course of your life? How did you go about making these actions into habits? How can you use these experiences to make study a regular habit?

2. What does it mean to you to rest in God? How can study help you to find rest in God? How does rest influence your faith?

3. What does character mean to you? How do you think study can shape your character?

4. Why is it important to study with a group? How does a group help you stay diligent with your studies? Who do you know who might want to study with you? When can you meet with them?

NOTES

CHAPTER ONE

1 https://www.goodreads.com/quotes/6806-the-more-that-you-read-the-more-things-you-will.

2 This quotation, widely attributed to Johann Wolfgang von Goethe, is an adaptation of material taken from Goethe's writings. See http://thingfinder.blogspot.com/2017/04/the-moment-one-definitely-commits.html, accessed September 12, 2019.

3 For "abomination," see https://deadspin.com/the-philadelphia-76ers-are-a-godless-abomination-1659664618. For "atrocity," see https://twitter.com/stephenasmith/status/667418053265793028. For the "short-term gains" quotation, see https://qz.com/890093/trust-the-process-how-three-years-of-losing-on-purpose-turned-the-philadelphia-76ers-into-winners/.

4 Susan Winlow, "Prison education program allows inmates to keep learning," *Daily Republic* (October 5, 2014).

5 http://www.nationaldefensemagazine.org/articles/2012/5/1/2012may-too-much-information-not-enough-intelligence

6 Albert Einstein, T*he Expanded Quotable Einstein*, Alice Calaprice, ed. (Princeton University Press, 2000), 281.

7 All direct quotations are from a 2013 interview on NBA TV with Ahmad Rashad. See https://www.youtube.com/watch?v=hXdj8scRdFE.

CHAPTER TWO

1 "Dirt Poor: Have Fruits and Vegetables Become Less Nutritious?" *Scientific American* (April 27, 2011); https://www.scientificamerican.com/article/soil-depletion-and-nutrition-loss/, accessed September 12, 2019.

2 Jonathan Edwards, "The Importance and Advantage of a Thorough Knowledge of Divine Truth" in *The Works of President Edwards in Four Volumes* . . . (New York: Leavitt, Trow & Co., 1844–47), vol. 4, 2.

3 Edwards, 6.

4 All quotations in this section are taken from Wesley's extended response to this question. John Wesley, Minutes of several conversations between the Reverend Mr. John and Charles Wesley, and others, from the year 1744 to the year 1780 (London: J. Paramore, 178), 22.

5 See https://news.usc.edu/134580/internet-use-at-home-soars-to-more-than-17-hours-per-week/.

6 David G. Benner, *The Gift of Being Yourself* (Downers Grove, IL: InterVarsity Press, 2015), 22.

7 John Wesley, "Address to the Clergy," §1.2, *The Works of John Wesley*, Vol. 10 (London, Wesleyan Methodist Book Room, 1872), 483.

8 https://www.ministrymagazine.org/archive/2016/03/Why-young-people-are-sticking-with-church

9 Jonathan Edwards, "The Importance and Advantage of a Thorough Knowledge of Divine Truth" in *The Works of President Edwards in Four Volumes* . . . (New York: Leavitt, Trow & Co., 1844–47), vol. 4, 13.

10 Entry on "olive oil" from *The International Standard Bible Encyclopedia*, Geoffrey W. Bromiley, general editor (Grand Rapids, MI: Wm. B. Eerdman's Publishing Co., 1986), 586.

11 Dick Vermeil, https://www.espn.com/nfl/preview07/news/story?id=2973338.

NOTES

CHAPTER THREE

1 https://www.gottman.com/blog/the-magic-relationship-ratio-according-science/.

2 Afro-American Spiritual, "There Is a Balm in Gilead," The United Methodist Hymnal (Nashville: The United Methodist Publishing House, 1989), 375.

3 http://www.marketwatch.com/story/
for-young-workers-who-move-constantly-a-loss-of-community

4 https://www.nationalgeographic.com/magazine/2009/10/redwoods-earths-tallest-trees/;

http://env.cpp.edu/sites/default/files/P_LA6441_Exercise%233_RedwoodForest_Poster_
Kaihara.pdf.

5 C.S. Lewis, Mere Christianity (NY: Macmillan, 1960), 106.

6 Blaise Pascal, Pensees (NY: Penguin, 1966), 75.

7 For Dick Van Dyke story, see https://www.theguardian.com/lifeandstyle/2016/dec/17/
dick-van-dyke-someone-should-have-told-me-to-work-on-my-cockney-accent.

8 Tom Stafford, "How to Check if You're in a News Echo Chamber—And What to Do About It," Society for Personality and Social Psychology. http://www.spsp.org/news-center/blog/
news-echo-chamber

9 Based on Margaret Silf, One Hundred More Wisdom Stories (Oxford, UK: Lion Hudson), 89.

10 Based on Silf, 15.

11 http://www.pewsocialtrends.org/2019/02/20/
most-u-s-teens-see-anxiety-and-depression-as-a-major-problem-among-their-peers/

12 https://www.openaccessgovernment.org/mental-health-among-millennials/53137/

13 https://www.theguardian.com/society/2011/may/05/quarterlife-crisis-young-in-
secure-depressed; https://www.forbes.com/sites/brucelee/2018/05/12/
depression-diagnoses-up-33-up-47-among-millennials-why-there-is-an-upside/#75b2e5cd5061

CHAPTER FOUR

1 See https://nypost.com/2009/01/17/quiet-air-hero-is-captain-america/.

2 Angela Duckworth, Grit: The Power of Passion and Perseverance (New York: Simon & Schuster, 2016), 139.

3 During the Revolutionary War, 4,400 died; War of 1812, 2,260; Mexican-American War, 13,263; see https://www.battlefields.org/learn/civil-war/battles/gettysburg, https://www.va.gov/
opa/publications/factsheets/fs_americas_wars.pdf.

4 A Report to the Secretary of War of the Operations of the Sanitary Commission (Washington, DC: McGill & Witherow, 1861), 93.

5 Bruce Catton, Reflections on the Civil War, John Leekley, ed. (Doubleday, 1982), 43.

6 http://wesley.nnu.edu/john-wesley/john-wesleys-notes-on-the-bible/
notes-on-the-second-epistle-general-of-st-peter/.

7 For ILO quotation, see https://www.ilo.org/global/about-the-ilo/newsroom/news/
WCMS_071326/lang--en/index.htm.

8 For American Heart Association statistic, see https://www.heart.org/en/healthy-living/
healthy-lifestyle/stress-management/stress-and-heart-health.

9 See https://www.webcitation.org/62C0yfhcJ?url=http://duende.uoregon.edu./~hsu/blogfiles/
Shoda%2CMischel%2C%26Peake%281990%29.pdf

10 Arthur Rubinstein, cited in Jeffrey, Brooks, The Rhinoceros Tale (NY: Writer's Showcase, 2002), 69.

11 Victor Hugo, *Les Miserables* (Hertfordshire, UK: Wordsworthy Classics, 1994), 47)

12 Hugo, 52.

13 Hugo, 72.

14 Hugo, 73.

15 Johann Wolfgang von Goethe quoted in John Stuart Blackie, *The Wisdom of Goethe* (Edinburgh Scotland: William Blackwood & Sons, 1883), 171.

16 See https://www.umcdiscipleship.org/resources/everyday-disciples-john-wesleys-22-questions

Made in the USA
Las Vegas, NV
15 May 2021